Arts and Crafts for Lent

From Mardi Gras to Passiontide With Prayers and Blessings for Family, School, and Church

written and illustrated by

Jeanne Heiberg

PAULIST PRESS
New York · Mahwah, N.J.

Book design by Saija Autrand, Faces Type & Design

Library of Congress Cataloging-in-Publication Data

Heiberg, Jeanne.
    Arts and crafts for Lent : from Mardi Gras to Passiontide, with prayers and blessings for family, school, and church / written and illustrated by Jeanne Heiberg.
        p.   cm.
    ISBN 0-8091-3683-X (alk. paper)
    1. Lent—Prayer-books and devotions—English.   2. Children—Prayer-books and devotions—English.   3. Catholic Church—Prayer-books and devotions—English.   4. Christian art and symbolism.   5. Bible crafts.   I. Title.
    BX2170.L4H45   1996
    263′.92—dc20   96-29313
                                                                                                          CIP

Published by Paulist Press
997 Macarthur Boulevard
Mahwah, New Jersey 07430

Printed and bound in the
United States of America

Contents

Acknowledgments

Many thanks to all the great people who helped make this book possible: manuscript readers Nancy Harradine, catechist; Sister Joan Vlaum, director of religious education; and Chris Weber, director of catechist programs, Diocese of Albany, who gave an exceptionally valuable overview. Because they work at different levels, these friends were able to give feedback from different directions. I would like to express special appreciation to Nelly Brown Bunk and Minou Ledji for their considerable musical gifts and their willingness to advise, compose, and share in creative joys.

Thanks also to Trina Paulus, author of *Hope for the Flowers* and past president of Cornucopia, who appropriately gave ideas, information, enthusiasm, and feedback about wormhouses, and to Mary Appelhof, worm expert and author, who gave feedback, as did Mary Frances Fenton, illustrator of *Worms Eat My Garbage.* Mary Frances also, with Dr. Barbara L. Harris, collaborated with Mary Appelhof on *Worms Eat Our Garbage,* a learning resource for schools.

I am also grateful to fellow directors of religious education and to the amazingly generous and creative volunteer teachers I have worked with in New Jersey and New York; to Lutheran pastor James A. Hulihan, an ecumenical sounding board; to the late Mary Reed Newland, who loved and lived the seasons so vividly with family, friends, and readers; and to people who were part of Grailville Community College, Loveland, Ohio, in early days, who made Lent a rich, meaningful, and renewing time of growth.

Finally special thanks to editor Don Brophy, production director Theresa Sparacio, and Paulist Press for bringing a more-than-usually complex book to publication.

Introduction

Five-year-old Jabar cried long and loud; tears gushed from his eyes. The volume of voice, the power of emotion that came from such a small frame was amazing. His little body shook with sobs as though his world had collapsed. What caused this anguish?

The Power of a Magic Marker

Older children, drawn by the color and creativity, the arts and crafts, often sneaked into the Newark Youth Center Whole Language Room I developed. Big kids told me, with impish grins, "I'm only eight," to try to get in. Fourteen-year-old Hareem was even smarter; he offered to help with the class. He liked talking to the younger children about what they were doing. However, when Jabar, totally immersed in his creative work, ignored pleas to put away and clean up, Hareem zealously grabbed the marker out of his hand, setting off emotional fireworks.

The strength of Jabar's reaction to the loss of a magic marker told me how important that tool was to him, how much he needed it. His parents had been addicts and alcoholics—his mother while pregnant—and Jabar may have been neglected or abused. There was a lot in him that needed to be expressed and healed. Something vital had been interrupted when he lost the marker. It took a long time for him to work through his feelings, even with offers of more markers. Because it involved him with some-thing healing and happy, the marker became extremely important to Jabar.

Jabar had other days of uninterrupted expression; Hareem helped them to happen when I explained how important the experience was for Jabar. All the children who came to the Whole Language Room grew visibly in learning skills and often in other ways also. Good things happened emotionally and intellectually when they became totally engaged in creative expression. They grew in much needed self-esteem; took pride in accomplishing; made important ideas part of their mental outlook; and learned to love learning.

More Involvement Means More Learning

In Newark, the need for self-esteem, emotional outlets and intellectual accomplishment was especially evident, but it is true for all children. All learn more when they are involved, when their imagination and creativity are engaged. Connecting an idea to an exciting activity in which people can express themselves helps them to keep that idea as their own.

The Atrium and Religious Education

Good parents and teachers want their children to have the best possible education. For people of faith, growing in faith is one of the most important goals.

Two great educational leaders of this century had that goal in mind and pursued it with great success. Maria Montessori, who discovered how children learn during sensitive periods, intended religion to be at the heart of her system. She called this religious component *The Atrium,* after the courtyards at the center of Greek and Roman houses and the entrances to early Christian basilicas. *The Atrium* was to be the entryway to faith for children.

Montessori found that children between ages three and six are like sponges soaking up knowledge, eager to discover, and capable of enormous learning feats when the senses (sight, smell, touch, taste hearing), choices, and activities were related to a subject.

Her success in teaching secular subjects and the worldwide demand for her time that followed prevented her from fully developing the religious component that she had intended to be at the heart of her schools.

Another brilliant Italian woman, Sofia Cavalletti, picked up Montessori's vision and methods and focused them on religious education. By engaging the imagination of the child and involving the senses, she also had great success. Cavalletti's students understood abstract and spiritual concepts at an early age; they entered into a love affair with God and looked forward to religion class and church worship.

At a Cavalletti-inspired Atrium in Montclair, New Jersey, I saw wide-eyed five- and six-year-old children sit perfectly still as they listened to their teacher, watched what she did, and performed the simple actions she asked them to do.

The teacher spoke in a hushed voice about baptism, gave them baptismal symbols (oil, a small robe to handle), and let them pour water over their hands from a large shell. After the lesson, the children chose the craft or other hands-on activity that would bring the message home, firmly fixing it in their young minds forever.

Parents told me that their children now looked forward to church services, enjoyed ritual and prayer, sang the songs with gusto, and sometimes even liked to imitate the gestures of the worship leader. They were following the child's natural path to prayer with gesture, song, and involvement of the heart.

Happy and Effective Classes

Many Sunday schools, catechetical programs, parochial schools and religious education centers also have discovered the benefits of arts and activities. Ideas are reinforced with a hands-on experience that children enjoy and remember.

Because many programs rely on one-hour weekly sessions, this book contains projects that take only a few minutes or that children can take home to extend the learning time. This homework also supports parents in their important work of passing on faith.

Faith Building in Families

Sunday schools, bible classes, catechetical programs, or even parochial five-day-a-week schools are extremely important, but they are not the only places for building faith; the family is essential. Parents are the primary religious educators.

Home learning can be more relaxed and ongoing. There is more opportunity to make it what it should be: a joyful, lived experience. This can most often happen through celebrations of the great feasts and seasons, when parents and children can do things together.

Parents are busy these days, and shorter projects may also help them. I hope that most will be able to spend a little more enjoyable, quality time with their children doing faith-building projects. Parents know their children. Who better can rephrase an idea to fit their experiences, help pick out a color, show how to glue with just a dab, or take a tiny stitch that won't show on the front? Who better can enjoy what their children do and display it proudly for all to honor?

There are great rewards for parents who help children have such happy experiences. Some reasons, among many, are:

1. The happiness of the children increases their own happiness.

2. As they help their children grow in faith, their own faith expands and deepens.

3. They see their children grow in healthy self-esteem, and their own grows as well.

4. They foster unity and love between the children and themselves, and between the children and God; God blesses them, and their life is richer, more peaceful, and happier.

Community Building

Some of the activities in this book are also effective for times when many families get together and support each other as a community of faith. Bible-study groups, RCIA (Rite of Christian Initiation for Adults) programs, retreats, family days, and adult-education programs can all be enriched. At all levels arts, crafts, and activities bring ideas to life, flesh them out, and make them memorable, involving and unforgettable. Ideas can be said in only so many ways; then people of all ages need time to absorb them, act on them, and reflect and pray with them. Do not overlook these wonderful ways of building community, nurturing faith, and sharing traditions in a holistic and happy way.

THE SEASON OF LENT

In the Christian tradition Lent is a time to focus on the more serious side of life. Why Jesus came to teach us, suffer and die for us, and give us hope in his resurrection—these are things you learn at increasingly deeper levels each year through a good Lent.

You may get very busy during the rest of the year doing good things, but Lent offers the reminder to become more reflective and ask big questions, such as: How am I relating to God, my family, and my friends? Am I growing in love and service? Am I caring for needs around me and in the world? Are there any areas where the flow of love from God through me to others is blocked? Where I could love more? Meditate more? Balance out better the areas of love, work, recreation, and spiritual growth?

The most important question of all to ask is: Who or what is at the center of my life? Is it God? Or is it things, objects, my own ego, ambition, apathy, self-interest, or any other business? Lent is a calm, quiet call to refocus, regroup priorities, and renew.

A Retreat

"Going into Lent is like a retreat. During a retreat, you let go of what is only of superficial, temporary use in order to be open to what is real, to what gives the greater happiness. You get so much more in return than what you gave up."

This is the view of Dave and Aurora Protano, parents of four girls, ongoing catechists and youth leaders for all the ages and stages through which their children passed. I always feel secure with advice given by people who have lived the Christian life with young people through many stages on many fronts.

During a retreat, you get away from the usual business of life to focus on what life is. You become more concerned with being than with doing. Silence, prayer, and openness to God's word renew you. You return happier, more at peace, able to handle problems in a more loving and creative way.

Modern life can be extraordinarily busy. More than ever, people need quiet, reflective times simply to stay sane, to be more effective, and above all to grow in faith.

Giving Up Less for More

Lent is also a time of making sacrifices, giving up things. By getting rid of lesser things, you make more room in your heart for God's love and the love of others. You become stronger and happier as you do things to help your neighbor. Giving up a little, you receive a whole lot in return.

My friends Dave and Aurora illustrate this great Lenten theme. Like most of us, they really enjoy delicious food, pasta, good wine, conversation, and conviviality. Both teachers on limited salaries, Dave and Aurora are always ready to share good things with others. Warmhearted and generous, the Protanos always seem to have more than enough food and love, culture and creativity, ideas and élan for everyone, and visiting them is so much fun, so enjoyable, and so enriching.

Somehow, giving at the limited material level seems to result in greater abundance at the level of the spirit, heart, and mind—the unlimited level. At this, God's level, the more you give, the more there is; there are no limits. This is the level where it matters most.

Generosity and abundance at this level often seem to overflow into even the material, limited level as well. Those who generously share with others receive even more in return. The desert giving up, traditional for Lent, leads into lush gardens of abundance to enjoy at Easter.

A History of Lent

The season of Lent grew backward from Easter in the early Christian church. At first it was a few days to remember the Thursday last supper of Jesus, his Good Friday death on the cross, the Saturday of quiet anticipation, and the Easter celebration of his resurrection.

Because catechumens (people preparing to become Christians) were baptized at the Easter vigil, Lent began as an immediate, intense retreat, a final preparation for baptism. It was gradually extended until the days, excluding Sundays, amounted to forty, honoring Jesus' forty days of prayer, fasting, and temptation in the desert.

In time, Lent also became a retreat for the Christian community as it prepared to receive the newest members. It was an opportunity for those already baptized to be renewed in faith, to enter more fully into the baptismal mystery, and to put aside lesser things in order to come closer to God.

Because of its instructional goals, the season's readings and teachings grew into a summary of Christian belief. Themes of water (and no water—desert), light (and no light—darkness), and life (and no life—death) are extremely important. The baptismal signs of oil, bible, cross, and eucharist and the themes of death giving way to life and separation giving way to unity are also prominent.

Seasonal and Scriptural Signs

Because the death and resurrection of Jesus took place in spring, the rebirth of life in the Northern Hemisphere became a symbol of the new life he brings to Christians. The word *Lent* means "spring." The awakening and rebirth of life in nature became a sign of the awakening and rebirth to new life of Christians through baptism.

Before Jesus entered into his ministry, he went into the desert to pray, fast, and overcome the temptations of the evil one. Christians followed his example in order to overcome the influences of evil in themselves. Lent became the forty days for them to fast, pray, give alms, and make other sacrifices to prepare for baptism or the renewal of baptismal vows. In many churches, it is still a communal going out into the desert, yearly, to overcome what hinders you in living out your baptism.

Deserts are dry, barren places because of lack of water. Just as in Advent less light is used to get ready for Christmas, the feast of lights, during Lent less water is used to prepare for the life-giving baptismal waters. Many contemporary churches use cacti, sand, and rocks for Lenten decorations, and churches with holy-water fonts at their entrances empty them until Easter.

The entryway placement of holy-water fonts is symbolic. They are meant to be concrete reminders of the living waters of baptism, the entryway into the life of God and the community of God's people through the death and resurrection of Jesus.

You may want to use cactus and sand as Lenten decor in your home and empty out holy-water fonts, if it is a family custom to have them. However, many other crafts and customs, old and new, follow in the pages of this book to help you find something that will work for you.

Time spent with arts and crafts

and with music and prayer as people journey through Lent to Easter is time well spent on faith building for the family, the classroom, and the church community. May whatever you choose to do help to make your Lent happy and meaningful, a time of growth, and a prelude to a joyous Easter.

TIPS FOR ARTS AND CRAFTS WITH CHILDREN

As you engage your children in the crafts, keep their minds on the meanings and the materials and off the end product. As soon as people of any age start worrying about what their art or craft will look like, they tighten up. They enjoy and learn less, and the product as well as the person suffers.

People and Process Over Product

It's people and process that are important. Grappling with ideas and expressing them through work with their hands, children learn volumes and produce good things to boot.

One of the gifts we adults receive from children is the good excuse to be creative ourselves as we plan things for them. Take advantage of that as you use this book. If you plan to do the craft with a class or group, it's a good idea to try out the techniques yourself first. No one need ever see the results, but your knowledge and enjoyment will overflow to your children.

Whether or not you are pleased by the results doesn't matter; you will not be doing it for an end product, but for the joy and learning that comes with the doing. Keep firmly in mind *process and people over product,* and you will be surprised at how good the products turn out to be.

If you are doing the craft on your own to deepen Lenten meanings for yourself, the same principles apply. Enjoy the process and the materials; think about the meanings and how they are being embodied in what you do.

Without stirring up worry about how things will look or focusing on the end product, it's good to encourage care for a craft and pride in good workmanship. Watch for when someone does something well and point this out, preferably with honest enthusiasm. Create a climate of warmth, encouragement, and appreciation. Remember that there are no wrong ways when it comes to arts and crafts; there is only "do your best" and "find your own best way." You can encourage children, and yourself, by saying: "You can't make a mistake in art; there are so many ways to express things and to share ideas visually. Everyone can find his or her own special way."

Patterns are given in the book to start people off; however, many people, once their confidence is raised, will make their own wonderful designs. This is to be encouraged. Give people all the choices that are practical and possible within the structure of theme, size, and materials you set up for a project. They may choose which figure or symbol they will do, how they will interpret it, what color they will use, and what details they will add. Best of all, they may create their own patterns; provide plain white paper or newsprint and pencils for this purpose.

The more of their own vision people put into a project, the more they grapple to express meaning with minds, hearts, hands, and eyes, the more they will be involved. This, along with the enjoyment of working together on a meaningful project, will help you and others to grow during Lent.

TIPS FOR BLESSINGS AND RITUALS WITH CHILDREN

Prayer celebrations, blessings, and rituals in the family or classroom should be different from those in church. Make them less formal, more fun, involving, and, whenever possible, geared to the immediate interests of the people who will take part.

Give children responsibilities and things to do. This can range from carrying a bible or alleluia banner to lighting a candle or reading a passage of scripture. The more you involve them, the happier they will feel about this kind of family get-together or class activity.

Ask children, as they are able, to help prepare for a ritual by looking up an appropriate scripture passage, choosing a song, writing a prayer or poem, and doing a craft.

Use movement when possible: through the house, around the classroom, or into the hall and back. Remember that in church liturgies and services people of different faiths sit, stand, kneel, genuflect, sign themselves with the cross, sing, and give verbal responses. The prayer leader in some services gives sweeping gestures, praying with arms raised high or extended out to the people; children have been known to enjoy some of these. They follow a great tradition; the *orans,* a female figure with arms raised high, was the symbol of the praying church for early Christians. *Orans* figures have been found in catacomb art; they go back a long way.

Some gesture meanings to keep in mind: Arms up with hands ready to receive—not clenched into hostile fists—express praise and openness. The Aramaic word for prayer came from *unclenched fist.* Sitting means relaxed, trusting receptivity and listening, while standing says we are ready to take action for God, to do what is right. Processing also says we are joyful in our beliefs, willing to proclaim and live them publicly. Kneeling, bowing, and genuflecting all express wonder, awe, adoration, respect, contrition, asking, and requesting. Kissing, hugging, and handshaking are gestures of affection, friendship, and support that most children love. They are the external signs, the seals of authenticity on our wish to live out the peace, justice, and love of Christ in our lives.

See how various prayer stances and gestures are received by your young people when you incorporate them into prayer at home or in the classroom. A sure winner is the signing of each child and family member with the sign of the cross on his or her forehead, perfect for night prayers, especially during Lent. This is tradition both in monasteries, with signing by the abbot or abbess, and in European homes, where a parent made the sacramental gesture.

When adults use different actions and sacramental gestures, young minds absorb and retain a great deal. Sofia Cavalletti stressed separating word and gesture to allow the action to speak for itself in its own time and space. Make the sign of the cross on the forehead in silence; say any words of blessing just before or after. Stop speaking while you light a candle, place a bible, or bless a child with a cross sign on the forehead or a hand on the head or shoulder.

Gauge the attention span of your group; have shorter times of prayer for younger children, unless you have them move or do something very interesting. Keep a few extra gestures up your sleeve to bring out when you notice restlessness. Better still, plan variety and movement into the prayer to keep young minds involved. There are many ways to pray, and God loves them all when they come from the heart.

Music, Imagery, and Stillness

Music and song will also help you to involve children in prayer; see the music section at the end of the book, where you will find some songs by Nelly Brown Bunk and listings of other sources for this important part of prayer. Use taped music as a background if singing is not for your group.

Along with moving and singing, have quiet times of stillness; peace is one of God's gifts, and Lent is a good time to develop a preference for prayer. Feed children's imaginations by asking them to think of lovely spring things: seeds growing, soft rains falling, and sun shining on daffodils and fresh new green grass, and on the children as well. Then, while their imaginations are engaged with living beauty, ask them to thank and praise God for wonderful things, to talk to God in their own words.

Encourage joy and spontaneity in prayer; this, and the crafts, will make the season meaningful and memorable and nurture people of all ages in their faith.

FREQUENTLY USED TECHNIQUES AND MATERIALS

Because the same materials and techniques are used in more than one craft, information for some is given here; you may be referred to them in later chapters. At the end of this section there is a guide to where materials can be obtained.

Paper Crafts

Construction paper is a basic material, but typing or copy paper will work in a pinch. Be sure to have a variety of colors. Order mixed colors for family or small-group use. For larger groups, if you buy packs

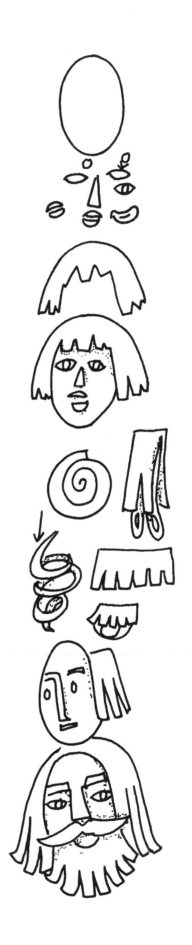

separately, order more white, yellow, light blue, red, and green; they seem to go more quickly. Besides the primary colors, get light and medium green, blue, pink, lavender, turquoise, purple, and magenta for a full range of expression. Packs of art tissue, mixed colors, will also enrich your paper palette and give another range of opportunity.

When a project asks you to glue and paste, this means that everything in the design, even the smallest dot for an eye, a line for a wing, or clothing detail, is to be cut out of a different color and pasted down. Young children sometimes need to be told that the design they are pasting is best done in a color different from the background so that it will be seen.

Use glue sticks when possible; they are clean and easy to work with. A light touch is all that is needed. This is even more true for white glue, which can get messy if used too generously.

Magazine Swatches

Free paper is available from old magazines that you, your friends, or your students' parents no longer want. Save them, go through them, and tear out swatches of different colors, plus black, white, and gray. Look for backgrounds, large cars with big red or blue areas, swathes of sky or grass, and perfume-bottle gold (just the gold, not the bottle). You will be surprised at how many and varied the hues you can find. Leave the parts that identify different objects; just go for the color.

Painting

Themes in this book that are related to other techniques (banners, sandpainting, etc.) can also be expressed in crayon, markers, and paint. Markers and crayons are easy to use and clean up; paint requires a little more planning. Some practi-

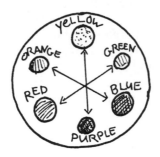

cal pointers follow to encourage a medium that children love.

Cover working surfaces with newspapers or plastic; keep jars of paint and water toward the center, where they will not be knocked over by inspired hands and elbows.

Provide young children with basic bright colors or mix colors for them. Give each color its own brush, so that a child picks out a color, paints with it, and puts the brush back—no need to clean it. Later, teach them to thoroughly rinse a brush in water and dry it with a paper towel or rag before they dip it in another color, especially yellow or white. Then you can give them a palette on which they can mix their own colors—an old plate, a safe piece of glass with smooth or taped edges, or an aluminum pie plate. Colors are lightened with white, darkened with black, and grayed with combinations of both. Mixing in a little of the opposite color on the color wheel gives nice subtleties; there is no limit to the interest and beauty that color provides as mixing skills grow.

Making Letters

The alleluia in the first chapter calls for letters, and you may want to use them in other banners and collages. A combination of word and image is powerful.

Ideas for forming ready-made letters from computers, newspapers and magazines, and copiers are given for the alleluia. However, you may want to form your own letters and develop a skill with many uses. Those made according to the following method will have interesting irregularities and design qualities, which is part of their charm. It will be a help, however, to have sample letters that you like in front of you while you work, so the magazines and newspapers will still be useful. Try to find letters that have some thickness. Block letters without serifs are easiest for starters. With some letters in front of you, plus paper, pencil and scissors at hand, this is what you do:

1. Decide on the height of the letters you want; cut out strips of paper that high to give the letters a uniform size.

2. Cut the strips into smaller rectangles in widths that approximate the width of each letter you will need: skinny for *I*; one-half to two-thirds the height for many other letters; a perfect square for *C, O, G* and *D*; wider than a square for *M* and *W*.

3. Looking at your letter samples, focus on the negative space, where the letter isn't. What shapes do you

see? Cut those shapes (approximately) out of the rectangle or square in front of you, possibly leaving more of the letter, making it thicker.

When you have cut away all the negative space, the part of the letter that isn't there, you will have an interesting, exciting, positive letter specially created by you.

Continue to cut out the letters you need to form the word(s) you want. Use them as is, for paper collage, or as patterns for felt or fabric (see the following section on cloth arts).

Cloth Arts

An alleluia for burying/resurrecting rituals needs to be made before Lent starts. Progressive banners and quilts are wonderful crafts to work on during Lent. They not only carry a teaching function then; they also carry the memory of what is learned throughout the year.

While the letter techniques for the alleluia may be applied to other banners, don't overdo the words, producing only a printed text. Banners should be visual, speaking through color, line, shape, texture, image, and symbol; use words sparingly.

The concrete cloth techniques given here apply to many of the other themes and patterns. Tailor them to your needs, interpreting them in other media and reducing or enlarging designs and measurements to fit your wall space. Progressive enlargement of a pattern may spread one book page out over several sheets; no problem. Reassemble them on a big piece of paper with glue sticks or scotch tape, then cut out the designs that run from one page to the next, so you have each in one piece as a pattern for the cloth.

For the quickest, easiest banners, use felt; there is no need for hemming or even sewing. You only have to cut and glue. You may also use woven fabric with fabric glue, or fabric stiffener, to seal the edges and keep them from raveling.

Fusibles, sold in the interfacing-interlining section of fabric stores, will also enable you to iron the letters to a background without sewing, though you will have to cover the edges with a binding, satin stitch, or paint. Follow the directions and/or experiment with smaller pieces first.

Though it takes longer, sewing a banner by hand or machine can be an especially enjoyable craft. Turning under the edges and stitching letters and symbols to the background can be done at home, or even in a class, while you explain meanings or have someone read a story.

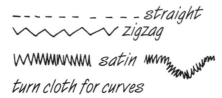

A sewing machine with capacity for zigzag stitching will enable you to simply cut the figures from the cloth, pin, and sew. You won't have to worry about turning edges under. A zigzag stitch will keep edges from raveling; a satin stitch, made by setting the zigzag very close (almost no space between stitches), will give you an added decorative element, an enrichment or another texture, whether you use matching or contrasting threads.

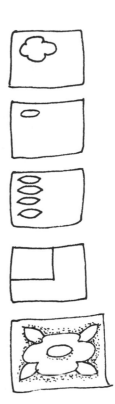

Progressive Add-Ons

Besides being easy, a felt banner background (or panel) provides a temporary flannel board for building a banner progressively during the weeks of Lent or all at once. A child or adult can smooth on the symbol; later, it can be pinned from the back so that it will stay up until and during Easter.

Velcro applied to the backs of symbols and to the places where you want them to go makes for even greater permanence.

With felt, you will need a piece of fabric the size of the final work; for woven fabric, add a one-half-inch seam allowance all around. Have at least one-half yard put aside for hanging/framing tabs and other trims to match.

Instructions below call for a backing piece the same size as the front so that you can line and hem at the same time. You may bind the edges instead (you will need bias tape or other binding) or allow an extra two to three inches all around to turn under and hem for the background;

add one-quarter to one-half inch for letters and symbols, and their parts—flower centers, eyes on faces, etc. Fine features may sometimes be added with a marker or embroidery.

You will need fabric pieces in the colors you want for these design parts plus scissors, pins, needles, threads, and other sewing tools. A sewing machine helps; fabric glues and fusibles provide other ways to hold your work of art together.

Fine (Pin) Points of Forming Symbols

When you have developed paper patterns that you like, the next step is to pin it to the fabric. Sometimes children need to be taught how to conserve fabric by pinning a design or letter to the edge, rather than in the middle, to allow other designs to be cut from the same piece. They may also need to be taught how to pin, so that pins not only go down into the fabric but surface again on the front. If the underside starts looking like a porcupine, this instruction is needed.

When you make the symbols, each will need its own small background piece, to which details can be attached. When completed, the entire symbol can then be arranged with others and with any letters on the larger banner background and attached by the method you choose. Sew/glue or fuse any that will be a permanent part of the banner (not those to be progressively added later) on the front of the large background piece of cloth, then add the backing.

To back the banner, place the front down, face up. Place the back-

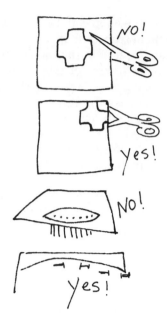

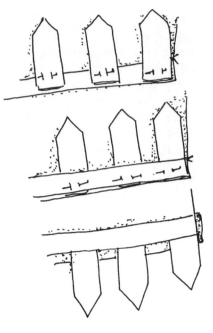

ing, face down, over the front. Pin the sides, then stitch them up. The banner is now inside out, with seams on the outside. Turn it right-side out, so seams are on the inside.

At this point you can cut down the backing on the top and bottom and fold over the front to form a hem in the back. Make your top hem wide enough to hold a dowel or rod for hanging.

You can also add other bands and/or tabs, top and bottom, to bind, hold a rod at the top, and frame. Instructions follow for bindings, borders, and tabs to use as described or to adapt to meet your needs.

Optional Borders and Hanging Tabs

When the banner has been backed as described above, cut two bands the width of the banner and about two inches high to form borders to frame the top and bottom. Place one face-to-face with the bottom of the banner, the other with the top, over the panel, so that all edges are even.

Sew each one-half inch in from the edge, then open, so that they form an extension of the banner, lengthening it at the top and bottom.

Cut two more strips the same

width by four inches in a contrasting color for a backing to these strips, and set aside.

Cut five hanging tabs, 3½ by 7 inches long (adapt size to the size of your banner), and linings the same size from colors that match or contrast nicely with the banner background.

Each tab is made up of two pieces of material the same size. Place them face to face and stitch up the sides. Turn them right side out, press, and bring both rough ends together to form a loop.

Place these ends at the top of the banner, loop end down, with the raw edges against the raw edge of the framing strip. Place the second, wider framing strip backing over the loops, exactly in place with the first framing strip, and carefully pin and baste. Turn right side out so that the loops are at the top of the banner.

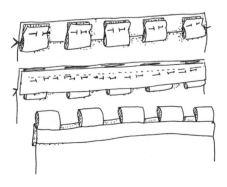

You may want to arrange the wider backing lining so that a narrow portion shows behind the loops to give extra color. Pass a dowel or stick through the loops and see how the banner will hang. Make corrections, then turn back to the raw edges and sew by machine. Turn right side out again and press.

Make five framing tabs, four inches wide, seven inches long (or adapted to the size of your banner), cut to form a vee at the bottom. Cut linings the same size in contrasting colors.

Place the tabs and linings face-to-face and stitch the sides and the vee at the bottom, leaving only the top open. Turn the tabs right side out and press.

Place the tabs on the banner with the vee pointing up and the top, raw ends of the tabs pointing down, even with the raw edge of the banner bottom. Follow the steps for the top, placing the wider strip over the tabs, pinning, and sewing. When finished, the tabs should hang down at the bottom of the banner.

The banner should have been backed, or the sides hemmed, before adding the tabs; however, these steps can also be taken now to finish the banner. Either way, the four-inch backing strip holding the tabs in place should be brought down over the raw edges of the backing, and its own raw edges tucked under. After tucking in all raw edges, sew the strip to the backing by hand. Pass a stick or dowel through the loops of the hanging tabs and tie a piece of string or yarn to both ends for hanging.

Variations

Add a symbol or decorative shape to the hanging loops and bottom tabs. Add more framing strips to the top and bottom and/or sides, or eliminate them entirely for simplicity. You can also skip the hanging tabs and loops and hang with push-pins, or pass a dowel through a hem at the top for hanging.

EARTH CRAFTS: WORMHOUSES

The amount of information needed for making wormhouses has made it more practical to condense instructions here; these are the basics. For further information, consult the following books: *Worms Eat My Garbage,* by Mary Appelhof, Flowerfield Enterprises, Kalamazoo, 1982, (616) 327-0108; and *Squirmy Wormy Composters,* by Bobbie Kalman and Janine Schaub, Crabtree Publishing Co., New York, 1992, (212) 496-5040.

You can order worms from Flowerfield at 10332 Shaver Road, Kalamazoo, Michigan 49002, by phone (see above) or by fax at (616) 327-7009. Appelhof also has a video and another book titled *Worms Eat Our Garbage.* I am merely a reporter on wormhouses, having been inspired by a serious wormhouse crafter who provided the information here; it is the only craft in the book I have not had time to try. But further help is available for teachers and parents who undertake this craft.

Materials for the Wormhouse

Five pounds of newspapers (Weigh them on a bathroom scale—try weighing yourself, then picking up newspapers until you weigh five pounds more.)

Fifteen pounds of nonchlorinated water, or enough to wet the newspapers until they are like a damp sponge (If you have chlorinated water, filter it or let it stand for a few hours before use.)

A few handfuls of garden soil, not sterilized, for living microbes from real earth

For the basic wormhouse, you will need a plastic container or a plastic-lined corrugated cardboard box or wooden crate; even a plastic bucket or dishpan will do. The size can vary; about twenty-four by eighteen by nine to twelve inches high is one workable size. For a cover, a piece of plastic or six sheets of newspaper will do.

Most important of all, a pound of red wiggler worms and, once they are in their house, kitchen scraps—mostly vegetable, no meat or dairy, and few fats. Use vegetable/fruit scraps, browning lettuce leaves, eggshells, coffee grounds, tea leaves, beans, old bread—anything but meat and cheese.

Decorating the Wormhouse Materials

Another box that fits over the basic box

Colored construction paper, art tissue, magazines

White glue and scissors for beginners

OPTIONAL: Contact paper in solid colors

Magic markers

Crayons

Tempera paints, brushes, water, and rags

With luck, you may have wood scraps and a parent, relative, or friend with a band saw who will cut it for you. If so, you can nail and glue a covering and paint it with white acrylic paint as a base coat and acrylic, oil or tempera paint for colors. All materials should be nontoxic to protect the living organisms that will work in the box. Use outdoor plywood, not the indoor kind that has traces of formaldehyde.

Crafting the Wormhouse

Tear the newspaper into strips, roughly one-half inch wide by a foot long. You can do this while relaxing and watching TV. You will discover that the paper tears easily in one direction but not in another, so try tearing down and across to see which way will work best.

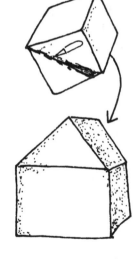

Soak the newspaper in the water overnight or until it is saturated so that it is like a damp sponge.

Prepare a plastic lining if your box is cardboard or wood. Loosely place a piece of plastic immediately over the wet newspaper and ready a lid for the top of the box. Check to be sure your worms will have air. A cover that rests lightly on the box will be okay, but with a tight-fitting lid on a plastic box cut holes in the sides and/or cover; worms need air.

While you are doing this, discuss the meaning of the wormhouse: why it is a help to ecology; why it is good to be responsible and care for the earth. Also discuss how and why we prepare our "inner earth" of mind and heart during Lent to receive God's gift of new life and help it to grow.

Decorating the Wormhouse

Before settling the worms into their new home, you need to decorate it in some way so that you and others will enjoy looking at it. Choose any of these techniques and gather the supplies.

There are lots of collage possibilities for the wormhouse. Paste construction paper over a corrugated cardboard box so that it looks like a house, apartment, or store. This will express your welcome to the little creatures who do so much for us. Use magazine pictures of houses to make your wormhouse look like a house or a garden with flowers and/or vegies. You can even create a whole landscape with the right pictures. You can also turn the box into a garden by cutting and pasting construction-paper or magazine leaves, shoots, flowers, vegetables, plants, etc., to express your love for growing things and the care you and your worms are giving them.

If you have a white or light box, decorate it with tissue paper. Paint a light coat of white glue mixed with water, half and half. Carefully place a design from cut art tissue over it. When the design is completed, brush on another light coating of glue to hold everything in place.

Any of the paper collages will do well with a coat or two of white glue mixed with water as a protective coat. Solid-color contact paper will protect plastic boxes and buckets, as well as cardboard. See "Paper Crafts" above for more collage ideas.

For a peaked roof on a cardboard box, turn another box on its corner and cut off the top corner so that it forms a peaked-roof lid. If you have a father, uncle, aunt, or other adult friend who does carpentry, ask him or her to help you design a box out of wood in the shape you want. Paint it all over with white acrylic house-paint. This will make a good base for tempera or acrylic paint, or even markers, to add the details and design. Any paint inside the box should be nontoxic.

Other possible media are paint or crayon over cardboard; cover your box—corrugated or plastic—with white posterboard or tagboard and apply any of the above—marker, paint, art tissue, magazine swatches, or photos—to create your design.

Working with Wigglers

Once the house is ready, the paint and/or glue dry, and the newspaper is like a wet sponge, its time to introduce your red wigglers into their new home with the following steps:

Fill the box loosely, up to two-thirds of the way, with the damp newspapers, and fluff it up; worms need air as well as moisture in their bedding.

Put your red wigglers into the box. They will immediately begin burrowing down into the bedding.

With one hand, pick up a clump of newspapers, and with the other, throw in some kitchen parings so the worms can eat. Do this in different places. Cover it well with bedding.

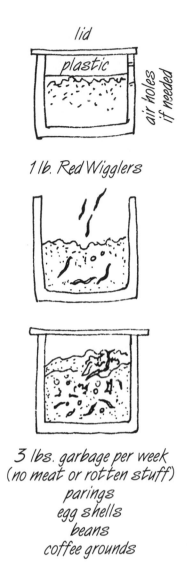

lid

plastic

air holes if needed

1 lb. Red Wigglers

3 lbs. garbage per week (no meat or rotten stuff) parings egg shells beans coffee grounds

From time to time, fluff up the bedding so the worms have enough air and check to see that the newspapers are moist, but not so wet that the worms can drown. Keep a sheet of plastic right over the bedding, but loosely enough so some air can penetrate. You can also use six sheets of newspapers or a piece of cardboard.

You are off to a good start on your wormhouse. Feed once or twice a week. Be aware of how much food is being turned into castings so that you don't overfeed, but keep the little creatures supplied with a continual flow of fresh garbage. One pound of worms will eat about three pounds of stuff a week. When the process is underway, you can go on

a three-week vacation and the worms will take care of themselves, even eating the bedding if necessary.

Reaping the Harvest

Gradually your newspapers and parings will become a fine, rich fertilizer for your houseplants and gardens. During the winter, save it in plastic bags for outdoor use. Use in a ratio of one part or less to two parts soil.

Every three to five months, or when there is very little bedding left, it is time to save the castings and give your worms a fresh start with new bedding. Once again, soak five pounds of newspaper in fifteen pounds of water. Push all the old bedding to one side of the box and put the new bedding in the empty space. Feed only on the new side for a few weeks. Gradually, the worms will migrate over, and you can remove the old bedding without ever touching a worm.

OR you can spread out a large sheet of plastic and put the contents of the wormhouse on it in piles. Clean out the house and fill it with fresh bedding.

Harvesting to garden

Push old to one side—castings go to plants. Fill empty side with fresh. When worms go to new side, take out castings on old side—put on plants (save in bags til spring).

Since worms don't like light, they will keep going to the bottom of the piles as you scoop off the tops and put the castings into plastic bags. Allow a little time for the worms to burrow down further, then scoop off more. Keep doing this until you have most of the manure in the bags and most of the worms in the piles. Then, return the worms to their house and begin the cycle again.

Troubleshooting

Wormhouses should not smell. If you leave garbage out in the kitchen it will, but fed to worms it won't; it will be covered by the bedding and turned quickly into castings.

If a smell occurs, check to see if the worms are getting air and enough, but not too much, food. If too much food accumulates, some can rot before the worms manage to eat it, while too little can starve them. If there is too much water, worms can drown. To guard against it, put in fresh bedding, add more air holes to the sides, or tape nylon screening to the top instead of plastic. The idea is to give the worms air yet keep the bedding from drying out or accumulating too much water. Cut draining holes toward the bottom of the box and place it on a tray to catch the runoff.

There should be no fruit flies or gnats if you completely cover the garbage with bedding. If you find insects hovering around the box, stop giving the worms fruit, especially citrus. Store kitchen parings in the freezer (or outside in the winter) for a day to kill any larvae before placing in the box.

Remind yourself and those who work with you that you are doing a good work for the planet, for people, and for yourselves if you also create good "soul soil" through Lenten reflection, prayer, and loving action for your inner gardens of faith.

WHERE YOU CAN GET MATERIALS AND SUPPLIES

Ordinary materials—construction or typing paper, cloth, felt, crayons, and markers are available at discount stores (Ames, K-Mart, Walmart, drug superstores); some of these even have craft sections. Craft, fabric, and floral-supply stores offer more. If you can't find things there, the following mail-order catalogues will help.

Dick Blick
Product Information:
1-800-933-2542
To Order:
1-800-447-8192
Customer Service:
1-800-723-2787
East: P.O. Box 26
Allentown, PA 18105
1-800-345-3042
Central: P.O. Box 1267
Galesburg, IL 61402
1-800-447-8192
West: P.O. Box 521
Henderson, NV 89015
1-800-447-8192

Elementary Specialties
917 Hickory Lane
Mansfield, OH 44901-8105
1-800-292-7891

J.L. Hammett Co.
1 Paliotti Parkway
Lions, NY 14489
1-800-333-4600

Nasco
P.O. Box 901
Fort Atkins, WI 53538
1-800-558-9595

Chaselle/New England School Supply
P.O. Box 3004
Agawan, MA 01001
1-800-628-8608
and
9645 Gerwig Lane
Columbus, MD 21046-1503
1-800-242-7355

Sax
1-800-558-6696
P.O. Box 51710
New Berlin, WI 53151
P.O. Box 20511
Lehigh Valley, PA 18002
P.O. Box 5366
Arlington TX 76005
P.O. Box 2837
Rancho Cucamonga, CA 91729

CHAPTER 1

Entering Lent:

Mardi Gras and Good-bye Alleluia

The transitions from Ordinary Time to Lent to Easter are dramatic. A full six weeks will be devoted to serious, sober stuff, and we are, after all, only human. Some entertaining entering events are in order to mark the changes and render them unforgettable.

Mardi Gras permits a party before prayer to see people through the serious season. Making/removing masks and burying the alleluia are prayers that involve the senses. Both mark the seasonal change in visual, vivid ways so they are easier to understand. Making masks and colorful alleluias are crafts that, created in this context, become faith-building events.

MARDI GRAS TRADITIONS

Children are learning to play roles society expects of them, and that, in many ways, is necessary. However, they need times of personal expression to balance out things. Mardi Gras has always offered this opportunity to people of all ages.

Of course, the excesses of Rio and New Orleans are not for a Christian home, class, school or church. However, a little fun and letting off steam are part of a great tradition.

In past times, serious people went without meat during all of Lent, except for Sundays. They also gave up butter, eggs, cream, milk, and anything sweet, fancy, and rich.

"Carnival sets free for a time our negative, irrational, and unacceptable aspects and . . . gives warning what global disasters the unconscious is able to create if left separate from our conscious selves. But through the ceremonies of its ritual action, it also allows us to recognize the vulnerable beauty of our human condition."

— **Gertrud Mueller Nelson**
To Dance with God

Because rich foods had to be out of the kitchen by Ash Wednesday, people tried to use them up beforehand, especially on the last day, Tuesday. *Mardi Gras* means "fat Tuesday." Pancakes and donuts were favorite foods to use up the remaining fats.

It was the time to have fun, to dress fantastically, and to get over-exuberant spirits, mischief, and naughtiness out of your system before settling into Lent.

The use of masks grew so that another side of your personality could emerge, one that is less reasonable and rational than the practical you of everyday. When you get to express your crazier side, you might not want your neighbors to know who that silly person is!

Gertrud Mueller Nelson, in her book *To Dance with God* (Paulist Press, 1986), calls the celebration Carnival and explains it as a brief compensatory time for the darker, wilder places of the human soul. The compensation is not only for the coming rigors of Lent but for the year-round restrictions society places on the inner, unconscious, shadow side of the person.

It's not proper or practical to express too much of your crazy side during work or school hours, unless your job is to be a clown. But Carnival turns everything upside down, and anyone can be a clown or king and wear any kind of wild or gorgeous costume, at least for a short time.

During Carnival, everyday strict rules are relaxed a little. Conventional rational behavior is temporarily suspended; the young and foolish may temporarily take over from the older, wiser rulers as they take on the roles of king and queen of Carnival.

You can help your people celebrate Mardi Gras and add pizazz to the party with mask making. Afterward, choose a king and queen of Carnival. Draw lots or see who makes the craziest, silliest masks. Have special chairs and robes for the "royalty" and let them choose some songs and games. Serve donuts and pancakes, traditional Mardi Gras foods, or other treats.

Follow the party with prayer; people are often ready for something of substance after the silliness. The prayer that follows this craft has a ritual of collecting the masks that have been made. This action images some of Lent's purpose: to set aside things of lesser value that clutter the mind and heart so that you can be more open to God's love; it is in that love that you discover who you really are. The ritual also symbolizes readiness to give up the false, selfish self and find your true, loving self, created in God's own image.

"When drawing near to God . . . we are dealing with a joy that puts the child in peace, that makes him serene and calm."

— Sofia Cavalletti
The Religious Potential of the Child

MARDI GRAS MASKS

Materials

Multicolor construction paper or light cardboard, art tissue, and other decorative and shiny papers

Scissors, staplers, and staples

Glue sticks, white glue, Scotch tape, and masking tape

Magic markers and crayons

String and yarns of all kinds and colors

Newspaper (to protect table tops)

Optional: The book or tape *Where the Wild Things Are* by Maurice Sendak (tape narrated by Tammy Grimes), from Harper/Collins

Preparation

The materials above alone will yield wonderful, creative masks. However, as a fail-safe measure to get the creative juices flowing and to insure that eyes are in the right places and that the masks are big enough to cover faces, make copies of the mask patterns, one for each person. These can be cut from construction or tagboard, or serve as inspiration for crafters to make their own designs.

If the craft time is short or the participants are very young, have someone help you cut out the mask basics in advance and have them ready for the craft. If all the parts are prepared, people will be able to assemble them quickly, then make their own creative additions to the basic structure.

It helps to show some sample masks and to demonstrate different ways paper may be used. Be excited about the materials, the colors, and the possible shapes to inspire your crafters. For a large group, set up a buffet table of supplies, patterns or cut-out bases for people to choose from. A creative crafts buffet is as much fun as food. However, it's also good to have food, to play festive music, and to read/play the story *Where the Wild Things Are.*

Motivation

Ask young people if they ever have a hard time sticking to the rules, doing what is right and proper all the time. Some examples are: not talking out when a teacher needs everyone's attention to do his or her job; dressing neatly, staying well groomed, doing a good job on homework; studying; going to bed and getting up on time; eating

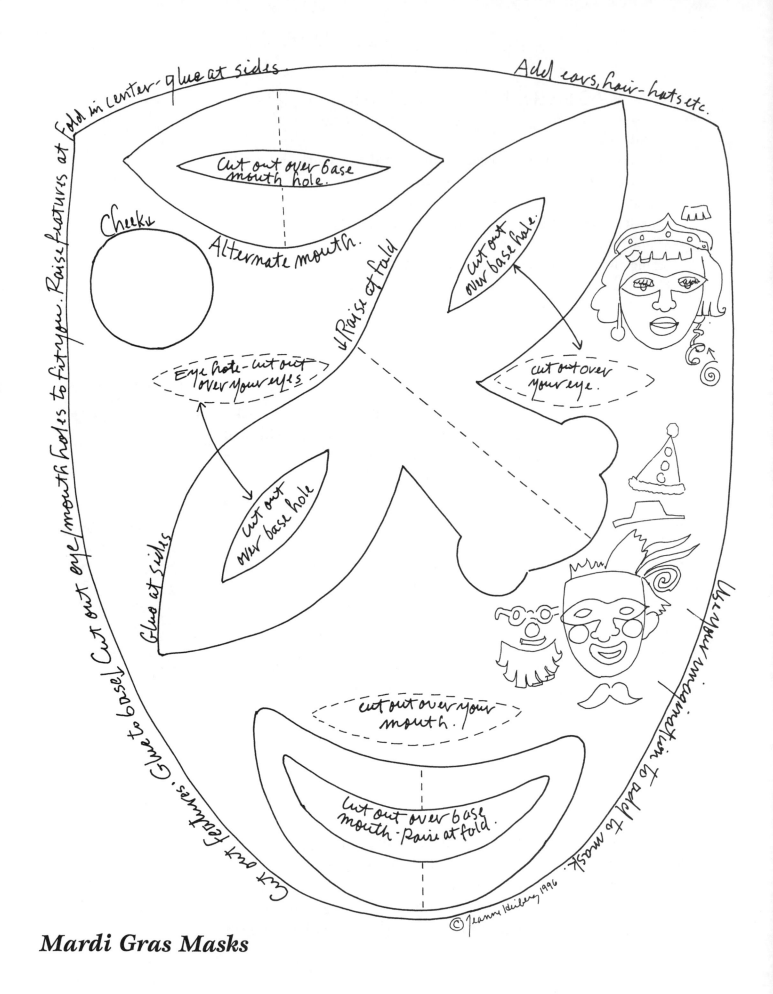

Mardi Gras Masks

healthy foods, avoiding junk foods; etc. Ask why these proper behaviors are necessary most of the time, and have some answers of your own ready.

Point out that in the story *Where the Wild Things Are* Max mistreated the poor dog, made a mess, and wrecked the wall with a hammer and nail. He misbehaved and was rightly punished.

In your own words, say:

We all have a little of the wild thing inside us. The church knows that we have to vent it a little just once in a while, but in safe ways that don't hurt anyone or anything.

Just before Lent, when people become more serious and extra good, we are given the opportunity to air our inside wild thing and get it out of our system so we can buckle down and have a good Lent.

A tradition has grown called Mardi Gras (Fat Tuesday) or Carnival, in which people have a party. It is agreed that everyone can dress and act in fantastical, crazy, and even silly ways.

In the past (and in some countries now) many people wore beautiful, wild, or crazy masks and costumes. They would have a big parade so everyone one could see and enjoy them.

In the story *Where the Wild Things Are* a dream carried Max to a country where all kinds of crazy monsters lived. For a while he had a good time carrying on with them. After a while, however, he grew tired and lonely and wanted to go home where people loved and cared for him.

So we, after the party, come back to remember that God loves us and cares for us. We enter into a season that helps us to experience this more fully.

First, however, the party. Look at the wonderful materials we have to make crazy, fantastic, wonderful masks that allow us to be whoever we want for a little while.

Doing the Craft

Demonstrate how the mask is made by cutting out a base as big as their faces, with eyes they will be able to see through, or by building on the precut bases you have ready. Show how to make the nose and mouth project slightly by folding them down the center and gluing them onto the base at the sides; also, show how to attach the ears to the sides with tabs.

Show many creative ways to use the materials: paper may be fringed, formed into spirals that hang down and bounce, twisted, folded to stand out from the base, etc. The idea is not realism but interesting color and shapes combined with imagination. Encourage people to experiment and find their own way of using the materials to create a unique mask.

Ideas for Follow-up Activities

View masks as young people parade around the room to music.

Choose the creators of the craziest or silliest mask/hat as Carnival king and queen. Let them sit in special chairs, with a special robe or throw over their shoulders, and choose a song or game.

Serve donuts or pancakes, traditional Mardi Gras fare. If it is difficult to serve pancakes with syrup, turn them into a finger food; spread them with jelly (peanut putter, cream cheese) and roll them up with a toothpick or clear plastic wrap to hold them in place. Or serve brownies, cookies, or other things most people enjoy.

Play the "Opposites Game." One person is the leader, who tells the group to do an action. Everyone responds by doing exactly the opposite. For example, when the leader says "Stand up," everyone promptly sits down. When the leader says "Turn your head to the right," everyone turns it to the left. Children enjoy doing this for fun with an authority figure such as a parent, teacher, or older sibling.

Perform skits and charades. Mardi Gras is a good time to express a different, less ordinary side of who you are. Derive skits from the trials and tribulations of everyday life, including doing what is proper and following the rules. Example: trying to get your homework done when everyone wants you to do something else and the dog wants to eat it.

I was once cheered during a stringent Lent by a friend's mime of a New Yorker in a subway car during rush hour, hanging on an imaginary strap, jiggling to a moving train, suffering indignities, not getting through the imaginary crowd at her stop, then doing double takes with a look of chagrin as she whizzed by all the local stops past her destination.

GOING INTO LENT

As a transition from Mardi Gras into Lent, try some of the following:

Briefly explain the meaning and reasons for the season of Lent and the opportunities it offers Christian people to grow in God's love.

Have a time of prayer to make the transition into Lent. As a ritual action, have everyone put his or her mask into a basket that is taken to the altar or prayer table as a sign of readiness to grow in greater awareness of God's love for us during the coming season.

Give people time to make Lenten resolutions; see chapter 2, "Resolutions and Sacrifices."

Save the masks for an exhibit during the Easter Season or return them to people after the prayer time, asking them to hang the masks in their rooms as a reminder that they are going to receive greater joys if they have a good Lent.

Entering Lent Prayers with Masks

HAVE READY: A large basket or box, several if needed, to hold masks; a gray (or neutral, muted color) cloth/burlap large enough to cover the masks; a simple, natural wood cross; a prayer table or altar, with a bible and candle.

LEADER: Dear (friends, people, children), we have been celebrating and having fun, and that is good. However, the greatest happiness, the greatest joy comes from awakening to God's love for us. During the holy season of Lent, we take time to grow in this knowledge. All the fun, all the material things in the world cannot take its place.

For a little while, we give up some of the things we otherwise enjoy. We clear out a space inside ourselves, into which God can pour gifts of peace, love, and joy. We take time to pray, to help others, and to learn more about God and Jesus.

As a sign of our readiness to give up some of the lesser, even silly things, to make room for the big treasures of God, we will place our masks in the basket at the prayer table.

This gesture may also express willingness to give up the false, selfish, self-centered self we all have, represented by a mask. You no longer need a mask when you discover the real you, the loving, kind, and generous you that was created in God's own image.

As you wait your turn, think about ways God has shown love for you. Think about something you can give up or a kindness you can do for someone during the next few weeks to express your real you, the kind and generous self that is in God's image. Then, when you put your mask in the basket, it will be a sign of wanting to give up that false, non-loving self so you can become, more and more, the loving self that is really you.

PRAYER: Thank you, Lord, for creating us in love and making us in your image, people of kindness and goodness, able to live in peace, light, and joy.

When we forget who we really are, when your likeness in each of us gets clouded over, when we sin and feel guilty, help us never to try to hide from you, Lord. Help us to remember that you love us still, and call us to return to you and to who we really are, your children, shining in your love.

ALL: Amen.

LEADER: As a sign of readiness to give up the false self that separates us from God and become more the true self that lives in God's love, please come up with your mask, now, and place it in the basket on the prayer table *(or give other instructions—to put them in the basket as _____ and _____ take them around).*

(Play quiet music while all bring up their masks.)

LEADER: I have here a gray cloth, and I ask _____ and _____ *(two names of younger people present)* to cover the masks with it. I also have a cross, and I ask _____ *(a different name)* to place it over the basket, on top of the cloth.

(Those chosen cover the masks with the cloth and cross.)

LEADER: Lord, thank you for all the happy, fun, even silly things in life. Thank you even more for the true strength and happiness you bring to us in Jesus, your Son. He helps us to discover who we really are, your children, loved and loving.

Help us to learn more about your ways this Lent and to give up some pleasures that are little so that you may fill us with joys that are great. We ask this in Jesus name. Amen.

Alleluia, Song of Heaven

Alleluia comes from the Hebrew *Hal-e-lu-Yah,* "praise Yah(weh)", or "praise God." It is a word long loved in the Judeo-Christian tradition, filled with promise and hope.

Symbolically, it is the song of heaven. It forms the sound that spells out our true identity as people created by God in God's own image.

Alleluia reminds us of our real home, heaven, which is not only our destination after this life but a place we can visit and experience in privileged present moments. Prayer, love, and their expression in the song alleluia are three keys to such moments.

Some corrections to an understanding of the word may need to be made. Tradition has handed down a picture of heaven as a place where we will forever sing God's praises. However, many people endlessly singing alleluia and strumming harps can appear a somewhat boring future. That is why a recent best-seller may have some good news about the song of heaven.

Embraced by the Light, by Betty J. Eardie (Gold Leaf Press, Carlson City, NV, 1992) was at the top of the *New York Times* best-seller list for many weeks in 1994. It describes her clinical death after surgery and a tour of heaven, where she saw colors more vivid and luminous than she had ever seen on earth and heard music emanating from flowers and cascading waters in a heavenly garden. She realized that the wonderful music, the perfect harmonies, radiated from the very being of things rather than from conscious use of instruments. Each element in a glowing rose, each drop in a sparkling waterfall and river was alive with its own intelligence and music. In this vision, music emanated from the being of things to form, with light, the very makeup of what things were. By their nature and being, all things made music and formed an intrinsic praise to God.

Since I read the book, this is what I picture the great alleluia of heaven to be.

The music of our being may be evident in heaven, but on earth we have to transcend ordinary, practical, ego-centered ways of thinking to hear its echoes. Alleluia, an almost nonsense song-word, transcends

"The Christian should be an Alleluia from head to toe."
— St. Augustine

Alleluia Banner

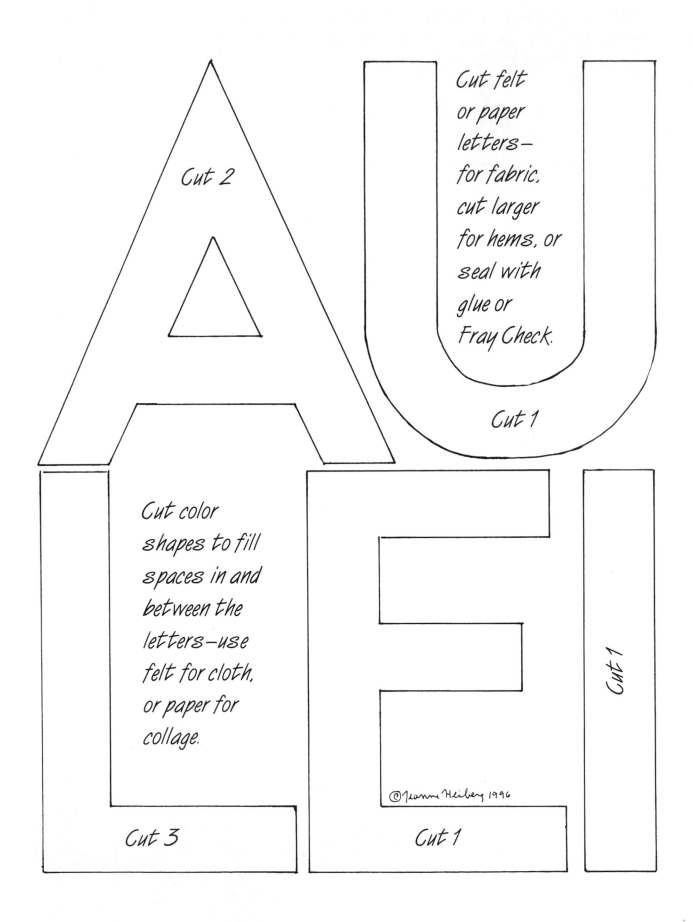

Cut 2

Cut felt or paper letters— for fabric, cut larger for hems, or seal with glue or Fray Check.

Cut 1

Cut color shapes to fill spaces in and between the letters—use felt for cloth, or paper for collage.

Cut 1

©Jeanne Heiberg 1996

Cut 3

Cut 1

logical thought to help you change focus. It becomes the symbol of who people of faith really are, children of God, created and destined for a wonderful future. It is the song of resurrection that will be sung with enthusiasm and bliss at Easter. Before then, however, it is put away so that during Lent you will experience the need for growing in God.

Alleluia says, "You have a wonderful future." However, to awaken to it, you have to put aside many lesser things that occupy your mind, heart, and body. Lenten practice has inspired people to give up unnecessary food, to pray, to forgive, and to put extra time, expense, and effort into helping others.

In a symbolic gesture, the wonderful word of heaven is also given up, put away for a while, to dramatize the loss of heaven's fullness and the need for God while still on the earthly journey.

A dramatic way of entering Lent may be seen in the custom of symbolically, sometimes even literally, burying the alleluia. After Mardi Gras, just before Ash Wednesday, is the perfect time, though it can be adjusted to when people are able to come together.

Burying the alleluia, however, has no meaning unless it is later unburied just before Easter services. Not one Easter egg should roll, not one chocolate bunny should be eaten before the song of heaven appears and is sung once more.

This unburying can be done in homes on Holy Saturday or early Easter morning before going to church. Classes can do it at the last meeting before Easter, in anticipation, or at the first class after the feast. Churches can make this a Holy Saturday ritual at the first Easter vigil or service beforehand. When the plants are brought into the sanctuary, alleluia may be woven in among them or hung nearby on a lectern, pulpit, or wall as an added expression of Easter joy.

Alleluia should remain visible for the Easter Season. After that, families have the option of putting it away or keeping it up for the rest of the year, until the next Lent begins. This way, it will become a familiar, year-round, faith-building reminder of who we really are: children of God made in God's image, made for heaven, with light, music, and joy as part of our very being.

CUT-PAPER ALLELUIA

Materials

    Construction paper

    Shelving or other long paper, such as continuous computer paper, with the track-feeder holes removed

    Scissors

    Glue stick, glue

    Two pieces of dowel at least one-half inch thick and two inches longer than the width of the Alleluia scroll

    Golden ribbon or yarn

    Optional: Large letters to use as patterns and/or samples of beautiful block letters from newspapers (I like the Sunday *New York Times*), magazines, books, or a computer

            Pictures of Easter symbols

            CD or taped music that includes the alleluia or music in an alleluia mood: chant, Mozart, spirituals

OPTION: FILL SPACES BETWEEN LETTERS WITH SHAPES OF FELT OR PAPER IN BRIGHT COLORS!

Preparation

Make copies of the pattern page of letters in this chapter or make your own patterns in the size and shape you want by using letters from magazines and newspapers or generating them on a computer. Use a copier to enlarge or reduce, if necessary. It's even more fun to make your own letters, according to the instructions in the Introduction under "Paper Crafts."

The words need not be written horizontally on a wide, short scroll. Break up the alleluia into a few syllables on each line to form a more conventional rectangle—twelve by eighteen inches, sixteen by twenty inches, or twenty-four by thirty inches—whatever will be a good size for your wall. The letter patterns in this book will work proportionally for any of these sizes.

The scroll format for the alleluia, whatever size, allows it to be rolled up for easier burial; however, it can unroll either horizontally or vertically for easier hanging.

Making the Alleluia

Cut out letters by hand or from a letter pattern. Paste the letters to a long sheet of paper to form the word *Alleluia.* Leave wide margins on both sides of the paper, or on the top and bottom, to allow room to wrap around the dowels.

Roll the two longer margins (on the sides, or on the top and bottom) over the dowels so they are covered and paste. This should form a scroll that can be rolled up inwardly from both ends. Tie the closed scroll with a golden ribbon.

Later, use more ribbon, or a cord, to hang the open scroll on a wall, or place it on a sideboard, altar steps, or other surface, weaving it between candlesticks, flower vases, or plants that will help it to stand.

Optional: Cut and paste on brightly colored paper to form Easter new life symbols: sun, flowers, leaves, baby animals, birds, glorious cross, or other shapes that fit between letters.

Variations

Have someone who does calligraphy letter it with a large flat brush or marker or cut out letters from magazines or newspapers to form the word. Use color swatches (not pictures or photos) from magazines to form the symbols or even the letters themselves.

CLOTH ALLELUIA

For something permanent on which to build your tradition, make a cloth or felt alleluia. It will become a real friend and save you the time and worry of creating a new one every year.

Choose gold metallic lamé cloth for the letters on a white background, or bright spring colors, all solids, or solids and figured calicos. Follow the directions in "Cloth Arts" in the Introduction.

Remember that time spent in making such an alleluia banner, talking about its meaning, and planning its burial and resurrection will help to build the faith of children in a family or class. People become more involved as their hands and hearts are engaged by an activity focused on an important idea.

Alleluia Good-byes and Hellos

The rituals and prayers that follow have readings you may or may not want to use. Even the youngest, however, benefit from reading scripture in the home; a line or two will suffice for them, while older children may be ready for more. You may want to read through the psalms listed here to find lines most appropriate for your people. Select reading lengths that will give food for thought to older children and adults, yet will not be too hard on the attention spans of younger participants.

Psalms 111-114, 116-118, 135, and 136, all of which begin with alleluia, are called Hallel Psalms. They have been sung for centuries by the Jewish people on especially joyful occasions, such as the seder meal of Passover. Most praise the goodness and greatness of God, some especially for the deliverance from slavery in Egypt (114, 135, 136). Others give thanks for a rescue from an undefined humiliation or danger; these are easily transferred to present situations (113, 116, 118).

Toward the end of the Book of Psalms, there are psalms of praise that end with an alleluia: 146, 147. A crescendo of joy is reached in the final psalms, 148-150, that both begin and end with the word of heaven.

Add readings from resurrection accounts in the gospels; however, in a very informal ritual or with young children no readings are necessary.

Materials
Alleluia banner
Box or cloth in which to bury banner
Place to bury (tree trunk, attic, closet, ground; if the ground is used, a spade and a waterproof box are needed)
Optional: Symbolic spade
Heap of cloth, brown, or natural burlap
Alleluia songs or taped music

BURYING THE ALLELUIA PRAYERS

LEADER: We have come to say goodbye to an old friend, the alleluia. This is a word you hear in church many times on Sundays. It is a word that helps you realize who you are: a child of God, made in God's image, in your very being a praise to God, a beautiful music, a song of joy.

Because of the distractions, hurts, pains, guilts, and just plain busy-ness of life, people often forget who they are. They become prisoners of things that are meant only to serve them and be used to serve God and others.

Lent is a time to give up things that distract you, that form a dark cloud in your life that keeps you from God, other people, and even from your true self as God created you.

There is a part of you that doesn't want to give things up, that wants to use things selfishly, that wants to hang on to envies and grudges and not forgive. This part of us wants to accumulate things for its own sake, rather than simply using just what we need and letting go what is extra or harmful. It is this side of us that sometimes makes Lent a time of struggle. But if we give things up, we are better able to grow.

During Lent the focus is on the cross, on what Jesus did for us. The cross is the symbol of his victory for us over sin and death, his triumph over suffering that ended our separation from God. Out of respect for Jesus' suffering we give up some things we like, even the alleluia. We put it aside, bury it, so that we can resurrect it with joy when we celebrate Jesus' resurrection at Easter.

READING: Psalm 112:1-7

SONG: Favorite alleluias, or see music section on last pages of this book, where you will find a special song for this prayer.

LEADER: It's time to say good-bye to our friend, the alleluia, to let it rest for a while, so that it will return to us at Easter full of enthusiasm to remind us again who we really are: loved children of God.

PRAYER: Lord God, our creator, as we bury this sign of heaven's song, help us to turn ourselves to living a good Lent. Help us to give up things that stand between us and your love, and walk with Jesus on the road that leads us closer to you.

We give up our alleluia only for a while so that we may make a more beautiful music in our heart and life when we sing it again at Easter. Amen.

LEADER: You are now invited to say your own good-bye to the alleluia, if you wish.

"Good-bye, old friend, we'll see you in a few weeks, so long alleluia, good-bye, we'll miss you, come back soon, etc."

(The alleluia is placed in a box or wrapped in a brown or natural burlap cloth. Indoors, someone may use a spade to symbolically lift a length of brown cloth or blanket on the floor so that the alleluia is placed under it, or carry it to a closet or attic; the whole group need not go with it.

With a waterproof box, you may actually bury it under soft earth outdoors, OR place it in the hollow of a tree, OR place it under bushes or leaves. Play music during this ritual or sing songs. After the alleluia is buried:)

PRAYER: Lord, we have given up for a time the song of heaven so that we may prepare our hearts and minds to be ready for heaven. Help us, in Jesus, to die to selfish habits that keep us from you and to live more fully your peace and joy. Help us to be renewed in your Spirit as we live this Lent. Amen.

RESURRECTING THE ALLELUIA

Materials
>   Previously "buried" alleluia, in a box or cloth wrapping
>   Symbolic spade
>   Heap of cloth, brown, burlap, to symbolize earth
>   Music (alleluias)
>   Flowers
>   Candles
>   Bible

Arrange a place of honor for the alleluia, with places to set processional candles and flowers.

OPENING SONG: "Welcome Back, Alleluia," in the music section

OPENING PRAYER: Lord, as we have journeyed with Jesus during Lent, we have tried to bury things that are false and of little value, that block us from your love. Now we are more open to your life and love. He brings us joy that will last forever. Help us to celebrate in peace and joy, singing the song of heaven with happy hearts. Amen.

READING: Psalm 148:1-6, 11-14, or Psalm 150

SECOND READING: Philippians 3:20-21

GOSPEL READING: Matthew 28:18-20

PRAYER: Lord, as we dig up the alleluia in celebration of Jesus' resurrection, help us to remember that you call us to new life in him. May we let no darkness come between us and our true life in you. *(Dig up the alleluia, or lift the cloth, and remove the box. Open it and take out the alleluia. As it is held up high:)*

LEADER: Let us greet our old friend, the alleluia, who has returned to remind us of who we really are: people of God, citizens of heaven in Jesus, who rose again and is with us.

(Encourage people to say their own hello if they wish.)

LEADER: Welcome back, old friend, we are glad to see you again.

SONG: Favorite alleluias, or see back of this book.

(Put the alleluia in a prominent place.)

LEADER: Thank you, Lord, for calling us to be people of the resurrection, in Jesus, your son. He has ended the separation between us and heaven and has won for us victorious new life. Baptized into his life, we can live in your light and receive the gifts you want to give us, peace, love, and joy forever. Amen.

SONG: "Alleluia, Sing to Jesus," *Today's Missal*

CHAPTER 2

Resolutions and Sacrifices

The Indian poet Rabindranath Tagore told a story about a poor man who heard, with elation, that the great prince would pass through his village. He ran to greet him, secretly hoping for a gift from this owner of fabulous wealth.

He joined the cheering throng of villagers, fellow farmers, and peasants, and to his joy, the prince stopped his horse before him. But his joy turned to sadness when, instead of offering a gift, the prince said, "What gift do you have for me?"

The poor man grudgingly drew from his pocket a single grain of wheat and gave it to the prince, who accepted it and rode on.

That night, when the poor man emptied his pockets, he found gleaming among the grains of ordinary wheat one of pure gold, his gift from the prince! He cried out in remorse that he had not given the prince all the grains of wheat he owned.

Tagore told a parable of sacrifice and giving that follows universal laws: What you give to God and others becomes gold, something of far greater value than what you gave away.

It is a longstanding tradition to make some sacrifices during Lent to keep this spiritual skill of giving healthy and strong. If the man in Tagore's story had honed his skill beforehand, he would have joyfully given bushels of wheat and received bushels of gold in return. Tagore's parable prince is a symbol of God, who is never outdone in generosity.

A BOOT CAMP FOR LIFE

Lenten sacrifice sounds uninviting until it is seen as giving up a little of what is limited, superficial, and unimportant to make space for real treasures with great, unlimited value. Most people start with only a few grains of giving, as did the farmer. It takes time and practice to build up confidence and trust, to realize that there is gold to be gained in giving.

You (or your children) may well ask the question, "Why should I make any sacrifices at all? If God loves me and wants me to be happy, why not do only the things I want to, why not get all I can, in possessions, enjoyments, food, clothes, entertainments, fun, and other good things?" Sacrifices, even small ones for Lent, do not seem compatible with modern concepts of comfort, getting all you can out of life, and going with the gusto.

Jesus, who made a great sacrifice, asks only little ones from us to center ourselves more firmly with him in God. For Christians, little Lenten sacrifices provide a kind of boot camp, a training, so that when necessary they can easily give up lesser things for a greater good and cheerfully handle any of the challenges life brings. The discipline of small voluntary sacrifices often enables a person to solve life's difficulties and problems before they become overwhelming.

"We discover God in Christ in the community of the Church. True Christian encounter includes the visible world, . . . and the God of this world with all his invisible reality. Christian encounter should include the whole universe."

— Anthony Bloom and Georges LeFebvre, O.S.B. Courage to Pray

A PATH TO SUCCESS

In order to learn the meaning of Lent and to experience the joy that comes from giving up in order to grow, children need something concrete to work with, a few simple resolutions they can stick to. Giving up things like sweets that really aren't good for them is a favorite among the children themselves. Other resolutions young people have shared with me are: not fighting with my brother/sister (big), eating my vegetables, saying my prayers, helping my mother/teacher/father, giving part of my allowance to a group that feeds the hungry, feeding the cat, and sharing my toys.

These small sacrifices, like the farmer's single grain of wheat, help children to build spiritual skills. People who learn to sacrifice a few smaller indulgences and keep God at the center of their vision more often succeed at whatever they turn their hands, time, and talents to. Success brings them more spiritual, intellectual, and even material

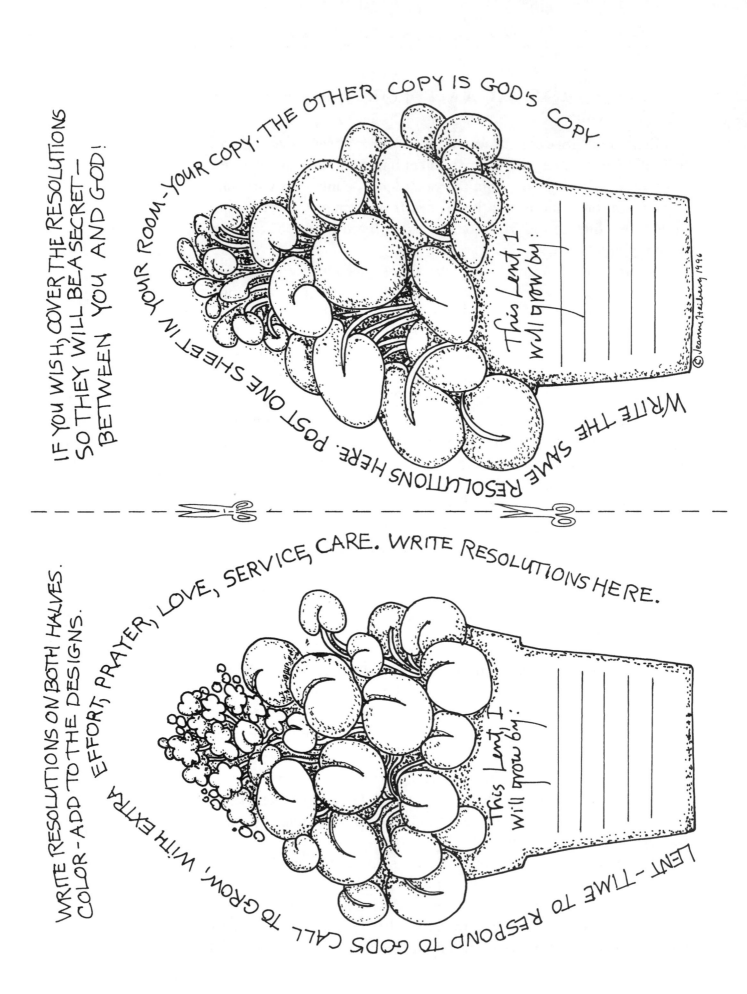

IF YOU WISH, COVER THE RESOLUTIONS SO THEY WILL BE A SECRET— BETWEEN YOU AND GOD!

WRITE IN YOUR ROOM—YOUR COPY. THE OTHER COPY IS GOD'S COPY.

WRITE THE SAME RESOLUTIONS HERE. POST ONE SHEET IN YOUR ROOM—

This Lent, I will grow by:

© Jeanne Heiberg 1996

CARE. WRITE RESOLUTIONS HERE.

EFFORT, PRAYER, LOVE, SERVICE,

WRITE RESOLUTIONS ON BOTH HALVES. COLOR—ADD TO THE DESIGNS.

LENT—TIME TO RESPOND TO GOD'S CALL TO GROW, WITH EXTRA

This Lent, I will grow by:

goods. They end up enjoying more and having more good things to share with others.

Scott Peck is the author of *The Road Less Traveled,* a book that has been on the *New York Times* best-seller list for years. According to Peck, the people who succeed in life are those who can put off immediate gratification and do the difficult and necessary tasks first.

First homework, then later perhaps a little TV to relax; first clean up your room or the garage, then go to the mall with your friends and have fun. Without this kind of discipline, the tasks never get done; grades go down and life becomes a mess.

For young people, voluntary sacrifices during Lent make the difficult lessons of life easier and more valuable as learning experiences. They often even eliminate the likelihood of harsher experiences you would prefer they didn't have.

PRINCIPLES OF LENTEN SACRIFICES

Lenten sacrifices are not meant to make life dour and miserable but happier and more productive. To make the most of them, Lenten sacrifices should be:

1. Decided upon with prayer, and concerning anything serious, in consultation with others, the wisest people that you know.

2. Made in the context of giving up lesser things for a greater good, with a constant focus on the good to be gained.

3. Done for love of God, other people, and your true (not your false, ego-centered) self.

4. Things that will not bring harm to you or others. They should, in the long run, bring about greater physical, emotional, mental, and spiritual health.

5. Chosen, whenever possible, because they will overcome a block to loving, giving, and/or growing, or because they will help others or advance a great good in the family/community/world.

6. Small in number, so they can be kept to faithfully but flexibly, according to life's circumstances. Love and obedience to God, parents, and teachers come first.

7. Voluntary, chosen by the person who will do them (even when they are children), and done with generosity and joy.

"Self denial is work and is difficult and irksome, and only love can make it a joy."
— **Gertrud M. Nelson**

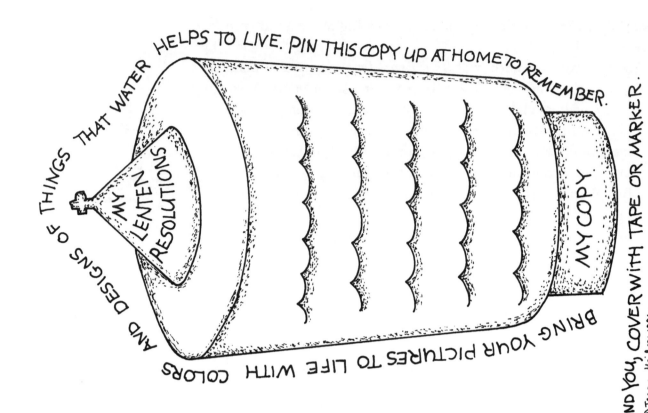

HELPS TO LIVE. PIN THIS COPY UP AT HOME TO REMEMBER.

THAT WATER

OF THINGS

THINGS

AND DESIGNS OF

BRING YOUR PICTURES TO LIFE WITH COLORS

MY
LENTEN
RESOLUTIONS

MY COPY.

© Joanna Heiberg, 1996.

TO KEEP RESOLUTIONS A SECRET BETWEEN GOD AND YOU, COVER WITH TAPE OR MARKER.

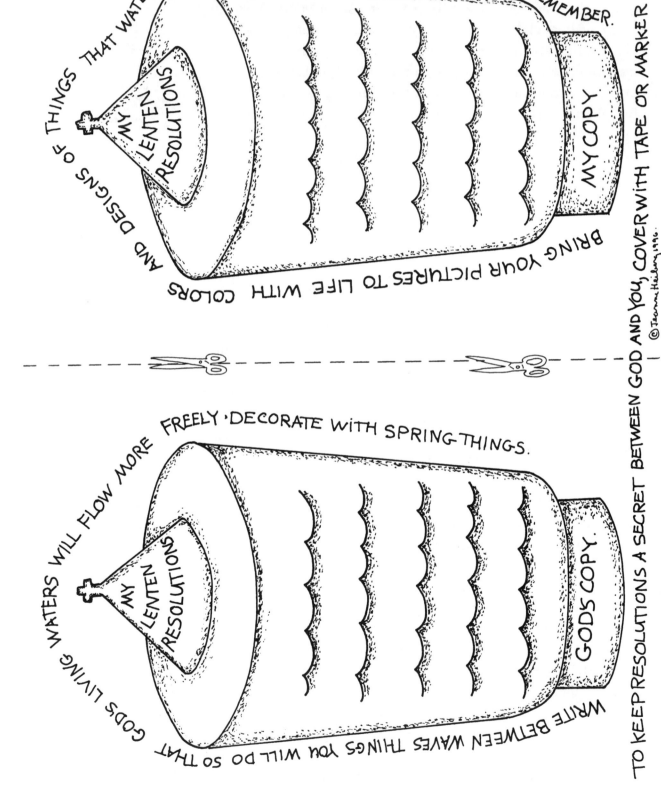

FREELY · DECORATE WITH SPRING THINGS.

WATERS WILL FLOW MORE

GODS LIVING

WRITE BETWEEN WAVES THINGS YOU WILL DO SO THAT

MY
LENTEN
RESOLUTIONS

GODS COPY.

BRAINSTORMING RESOLUTIONS

To help people see many possibilities for Lenten resolutions, try brainstorming ideas in a family or class. This provides group/community support and more ideas and choices. It makes doing the resolutions easier and more fun.

Begin with a prayer, asking God to help you pick out the resolutions that will best help you grow during the coming Lent. Then discuss possibilities with others; share ideas, including ideas you find in this book.

List one hundred things quickly, without evaluating. Include everything that comes to mind, even if it seems crazy. You are not evaluating, so nothing can be crazy.

Later, go back over your list and pick out ten of the best ideas. What will help you to grow and overcome blocks to service and love? What will most enable you to help others? Pick out three or four things you can honestly commit yourself to do faithfully during Lent. List them in order of importance to you.

Do Chores

Be Nicer to Sister

Obey Mom and Dad

Study More

Get Along with Tony

Less TV

Eat Vegetables

No Candy

Don't Fight

No Talking Back

Be Friends to All

Secret Lenten Resolutions

To dramatize their resolutions, provide a chart on which children can write down what they will do. To make it more fun and to stress the reason they are doing it, make double copies—one for God, the other for the children to post somewhere as a reminder. Give them something to cover up what they write, if they wish, so it will be a secret between themselves and God.

If children want to share their lists with you, fine! That's how I discovered some favorite resolutions. When this happens, encourage them and compliment them on how well they are doing as Lent progresses. Whether or not they share their lists, reminders during Lent may be, "Well, how are the resolutions going? Are you finding it hard or easy? I'm proud of you for taking them on."

Lenten resolutions charts in this chapter are provided to make resolutions fun and to serve as reminders. In families, all ages may share one design, but each will need his or her own copy.

In classrooms, go by grade. The flowerpot, best for younger children (eight and nine), puts the emphasis on growth. The font is ideal for ten-year-olds, who can better grasp ideas related to baptism. Save the cross for children eleven years old and up.

The Victorious Cross

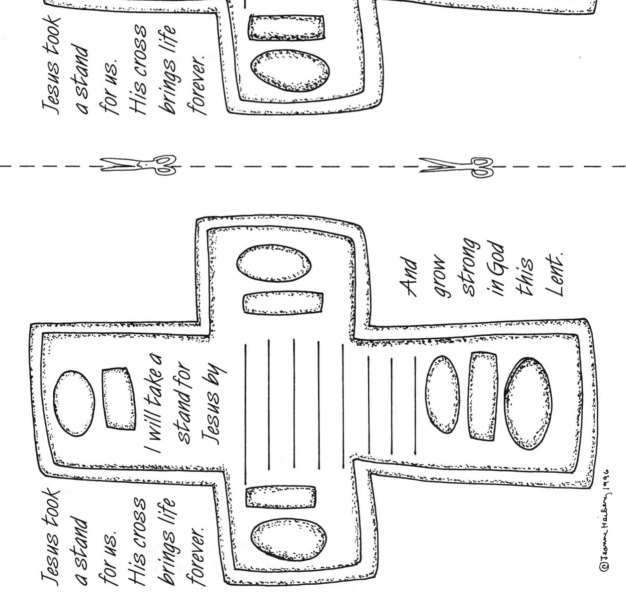

Jesus took
a stand
for us.
His cross
brings life
forever.

I will take a
stand for
Jesus by

And
grow
strong
in God
this
Lent.

The Victorious Cross

Jesus took
a stand
for us.
His cross
brings life
forever.

I will take a
stand for
Jesus by

And
grow
strong
in God
this
Lent.

© Jeanne Heiberg, 1996

Materials

Copies of a Lenten Resolutions Secret Chart from this chapter
and/or drawing paper for people to make their own

Crayons, markers, pens, pencils

Cover-up sticky tapes, labels, or substitutes: glue, scissors, construction paper (Labels in different sizes, colors and shapes add to the creative process.)

Introducing the Craft

Talk to children about the season of Lent and the reasons for making resolutions. See the prayers that follow for ideas that relate to the design you choose.

Doing the Craft

Ask the group to write the same resolutions on their two designs. Invite them to cover the resolutions up if they wish, then decorate them with crayons or markers. One will be God's copy, to be put into a basket (possibly during a prayer time). The other copy will be theirs to put up in their room, in their socks drawer, by their mirror, or anywhere they will see it every day.

Variations

1. Develop other Lenten themes for charts: a desert scene; walking with Jesus; worldwide needs; people of light; a plate with a wedge cut out, labeled "for the hungry and homeless." Have the children themselves draw these.

2. Have each person make his or her own collage design out of construction paper. Work in a flap to cover the resolutions.

3. Make a resolution wall hanging out of felt or fabric. Provide a pocket to hide the resolutions. All the members of a family may put their resolutions into the one pocket, and it may be used again year after year. Resolutions may be inserted during one of the following prayers.

Lenten Resolutions Prayers

The first prayer, with a growing theme, relates to the resolution sheet with two flowerpots; see Chapters 7 and 8 for more about Lenten growing. You might say something like:

In Lent, there is a tradition of giving up (voluntarily and lovingly) some of the things we normally enjoy. Spending more time in prayer is another tradition. This enables you to give more of what you have, both money and time, to help others, especially those who are sick, lonely, hungry, or suffering. This also helps you to become your best self. You make more room for God in your thoughts, heart, and mind; you become more like Jesus, a true son of God, made in his Father's image. Your talent develops. As a human and as a Christian, you grow.

To help you follow in this tradition and to make it fun, I have this double picture of a growing plant, with spaces for your Lenten resolutions.

Write in the same resolutions on both plants, then cut them apart. Cover one over with labels or marker if you wish, so that it can be a secret between you and God. Later, "God's copy" will go up on the (prayer table, altar).

Keep the other half. Post it where you can see it every day. It will be your reminder, so your resolutions will help you to grow during Lent.

GROWING:
A GARDEN PRAYER AND ART FORM

Materials
Paper, pencils, crayons, markers
Optional: The flower pot Lenten resolutions chart

IMAGERY MEDITATION

Close your eyes and relax. Imagine yourself in a beautiful, green garden, fresh from a recent rain, sparkling with the colors of many flowers. Soft breezes move the flowers on their stems in a stately dance; butterflies with brilliant wings fly from flower to flower.

Vegetables grow here too; there is a golden orange pumpkin peeking out from under a broad, green leaf. A vine growing yellow squash reaches a tendril out over a garden path, and rich ruddy tomatoes ripen in the sun.

The sun is shining down on all the abundant life in this garden, helping everything to grow and making the garden a happy place to be.

The same warm sun is shining down on you. Feel it warm and pleasant on your shoulders and arms. It's like the sun of God's good love all around you, a part of you, helping you to grow to be the best self you can be.

Thank God for creating you the good, beautiful person you are, made in God's own image to be loving, kind, creative, and good.

Ask God to continue to help you to grow to your true, your best possible self.

Ask God to help you to choose things to do this Lent that will help that growth. Be open to ideas that will help you to love more, give to others, and help the people around you and even those far away. Think about when you can have moments of being close to God.

Pray on your own for a while and listen quietly to what comes into your heart and your mind's eye. *(Allow some quiet time, depending on age range.)*

Thank God again for creating you in love to be a wonderful human being, capable of helping others, able to live in peace and happiness.

Open your eyes and pick up your pencils and crayons. Write and draw what you heard and saw in your prayer garden. *(You may add flower pot resolutions chart for people to fill out. Have them place half in a basket on the prayer table when they are ready, or save it for a group prayer.)*

GROWING PRAYER FOR GROUPS

Prepare a prayer table with a basket or beautiful box, a bible, a plant, a cross, and candles. Have song sheets or taped music ready. Those who gather should have their written resolutions with them. Use the litany prayers that best suit your group, write your own, or ask your people to write or speak the prayers. Select from readings according to your group, no more than one, or a few lines with younger children. See further song suggestions and ideas for prayers at the end of Chapter 7.

OPENING SONG: "Seed Scattered and Sown," verse 2, *Today's Missal;* or "The Lord Is with You," or "Forgiveness Prayer," *Rise Up and Sing,* Oregon Catholic Press

OPENING PRAYER: Lord, in this time of Lent, thank you for bringing us together to know more about how you want us to live. Thank you for times to grow in your life and love. Help us to always respond to your invitations to grow in Jesus, your son, in whom we will live forever and ever. Amen.

FIRST READING: Psalm 92:13-16

SECOND READING: 1 Corinthians 15:37-38 (or to 44)

THIRD READING: John 12:24

We were created in God's own image to be people of love, light, peace, patience, kindness, and compassion. When we forget how we were made and how God wants us to live, we cannot be happy.

During this Lent, God wants us to remember a little more that we are like seeds that need to burst out of our hard shell of selfishness. Our good and kind creator wants to help us to grow into who we really are, people created in God's own image, made to love God and others in peace and joy.

Our Lenten resolutions will help us to do this. It is time now to carry them to the (prayer table, altar) and offer them up to God. *(Children go up to the basket on the table and place their resolutions inside, or those selected bring the basket to participants, collect the resolutions, then carry them to the table.)*

COMMENTARY AND LITANY PRAYER: When we remember who we are, children of God, and when we grow more and more in God's forgiveness, love, and care, then we also learn how to be happy. We become like plants rooted in good soil, well watered, reaching up our leaves to the sunshine. Kind words and generous, helpful actions are ready to burst forth from us, just like flowers and fruits that burst forth from the plants they grow on.

Let us together pray that this Lent we will grow closer to God and be fruitful in prayer and good actions.

The response to our prayers will be: LORD, HELP US TO GROW.

That we will keep our Lenten resolutions well, let us pray: RESPONSE.

That we will be kind and helpful to each other, let us pray: RESPONSE.

That we will talk to God from the heart in prayer and know that God listens and loves us, let us pray: RESPONSE.

That we will trust in God's love and always be ready to grow into our best possible selves through both the hard things and the happy things life brings, let us pray: RESPONSE.

That we will grow closer to Jesus this Lent and be renewed in him at Easter, we pray: RESPONSE.

LEADER: Quietly talk to the Lord in your own words for a while now and tell God how you would like to grow during this holy season of Lent.

Now talk to the Lord to ask how God would like you to grow, then listen quietly to what comes into your mind and heart.

CLOSING PRAYER: Thank you, Lord, for the happiness you give us when we talk to you and listen to you in prayer. Thank you for the growth in life you are giving to us this Lent. Help us to put good effort into our resolutions and into all the ways you call us to grow so that at Easter we may be more joyful than ever in Jesus, your son, whose life in you we share. We ask this in him. Amen.

GLORIOUS CROSS PRAYER

SONG: "Lift High the Cross," *Today's Missal;* "Children of Tomorrow, Children of Today," or "Building the Kingdom," *Hi God 4,* Oregon Catholic Press

LEADER: Lent helps us to learn more about how much God loves us. We learn about what Jesus did for each of us when he suffered, died, and rose again.

He makes it possible for us to know that we are his brothers and sisters, God's own children. He makes it possible for us to live with love, not fear, to overcome obstacles and difficulties, and to grow strong.

Jesus will help us make good resolutions and keep them so that we become a blessing to ourselves and all around us, and all will end in happiness.

OPENING PRAYER: Lord, you gave us Jesus to show us the way to you. He loved us so much that he took up his cross, suffered, died, and rose again for us so that we can be happy with you forever in heaven. Help us to be strong in Jesus, to live good lives, and to stand up for what is right. Amen.

SIGNING OF THE CROSS RITUAL: The cross is the standard of Christianity. It reminds us that Jesus Christ died and rose again, and promised his followers that he would always be with them.

Every Christian church has a cross where people gather to worship. A signing of the cross is a part of many blessings and prayers for a great number of Christians.

In the Eastern churches, there is a custom in which a mother or father blesses each child on the forehead, tracing a sign of the cross with their thumb. It is a bedtime ritual, before sleep, to help parent and child remember that God is always with us, taking care of us.

We will follow that custom now. As your (mother, father, teacher, big sister/brother), I will sign each person present with the blessing of the cross. When I have finished, I will ask (_____) to sign and pray for me. I would like all of us to focus on and pray for each person as he or she is signed. Ask God to help him or her live a good Lent and grow strong in God.

(As each person is signed:) YOU BELONG TO GOD AS A BELOVED CHILD (SON, DAUGHTER) *or* BE STRONG IN CHRIST, WHO LOVES YOU.

PRAYERS OF PETITION: Let us bring before the Lord prayers that ask for his blessings. Our response will be: LORD, HEAR OUR PRAYER or LORD, MAKE US STRONG IN YOUR LIFE.

That we will grow closer to God this Lent through prayer and good actions, let us pray: RESPONSE.

That we will be strong and fearless in standing up for what is right, let us pray: RESPONSE.

That we will stick to our Lenten resolutions and live as God wants us to, let us pray: RESPONSE.

That we will know how much God loves us and share that love with others, let us pray: RESPONSE.

That God will take care of all who are in need, and that we will help as we can, let us pray: RESPONSE.

That we will live a good Lent, celebrate a happy Easter, and be renewed with Jesus and the coming of spring, let us pray: RESPONSE.

LEADER: Let us take a few silent moments, now, so that you can talk to God in your own words. If you have any problems, any crosses, talk to God and Jesus about them. Listen to hear what solutions may arise in your mind and heart. God loves you and will always help you. Ask Jesus to be your guide.

SONG: "I Have Decided to Follow Jesus," Servant Music

RESOLUTIONS RITUAL: Now it is time to bring forward your Lenten resolutions and to rest them on the prayer table. If you have another resolution you would still like to add, think it onto your sheet as it rests in the basket and write it down later on the sheet you keep. *(Collect resolutions in a basket.)*

God gives us so many gifts, and our resolutions are a gift back to God, who will bless them and use them to strengthen us and bring us greater happiness. Will _____ bring the resolutions to the (prayer table or altar).

BLESSING AND CLOSING PRAYER: Thank you Lord, for hearing our prayers, whether they are spoken, written, sung, or hidden in our own thoughts and minds. Help us to be strong in the strength that Jesus shares with us, through the power of his cross and resurrection and everlasting love.

Bless these our Lenten resolutions as a sign of our love and gratefulness for all your gifts to us. Bless us as we live them in prayer, action, and service. We ask this in Jesus' name.

ALL: Amen.

SONG: "Lord of the Dance," *Today's Missal*

CHAPTER 3

Prayer, Fasting, and Giving Alms

Three traditional Lenten practices worth looking into for further resolution ideas and creative crafts are prayer, fasting, and almsgiving. They are part of the spring plowing up and preparing of the soil of the soul for new life. Gifts of increased peace, love, and joy come to those who wisely make them part of their yearly Lenten retreat.

The three are interrelated and hard to separate. The money from the food budget saved by fasting can go into a handcrafted mite box as alms, or offerings, for the poor, homeless, and hungry. Prayer offers spiritual nourishment that makes giving and giving up joyful, and Lenten meal prayers bring that nourishment into family life.

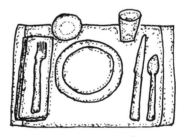

SPIRITUAL MENU

The projects for these three practices are also interrelated. A prayer cloth in a place set apart for spiritual nourishment recalls the physical food table. Try making it part of the dinner table centerpiece to remind everyone that kindness, listening, and considerate sharing during a meal offer spiritual food, and better health, for all present.

Spiritual menus also advance this idea, and decorated meal prayer copies are a further help. A mite box helps people to remember the reason for fasting and who it will help. It recalls the gospel story of the widow who put her mite, the little money she had, into the temple treasury. This is an encouraging story for children, who have less material goods to offer; they can give their all in love and kindness to others.

Prayer

Until eighty or ninety years ago, the fastest speed at which most people ever traveled was twenty to thirty miles an hour. Now people push speed limits of fifty-five or sixty-five miles an hour in cars and break sound barriers whooshing across continents in jets.

The frenetic rush of modern life lies not only in speed but in the amount of things busy minds have to attend to. More than ever, there is a need for prayer, meditation, and quiet. Eknath Easwaran, a meditation teacher from India, often quotes a bit of wisdom from his culture: "The fast mind is a sick mind; the quiet mind is a healthy mind; the still mind is a divine mind." He also repeats a line from a biblical psalm: "Be still, and know that I am God."

People need to quiet their minds from time to time for good physical and mental health, even to simply stay sane. They need to sweep away the clutter of trivial thoughts and concerns in order to hear the quiet voice of God within and to receive the great inner gifts of God; these bring far greater joy than any of the world's external goods.

Each family, each religion class will benefit from a quiet time and/or a quiet corner. As soon as they can stop their wiggles for a few minutes, children even enjoy learning to be quiet in prayer for a short time. It is an art, an acquired taste they will value when it happens in a kind, loving way. Imagery prayers are of special help.

A prayer environment helps all ages to enter into quiet. Many classrooms have a prayer table with a bible and a candle, and sometimes a plant, picture, or statue to add beauty. Many teachers who use a classroom only once a week bring their prayer table things, as well as their lessons, to each session.

In a home it's easier to set aside a prayer table or even to create a prayer corner. An icon or cross, if it is a work of art, will lift the spirit of the whole room and set the corner apart as a sacred space. Some people say they immediately feel a sense of peace when, headed for other tasks, they catch a glimpse of their prayer corner.

The prayer corner or table is the place for a family bible, always ready to be opened or already opened and inviting people to receive a thought for the day. Lent is a good time to teach children to look up bible verses themselves so that they can read them during family (or class) prayer.

As in the classroom, a few simple, beautiful objects (candles, plants, icons) make a prayer corner the place of peace that people need in their busy lives.

PRAYER

Fixing up a prayer corner is a good project for Lent, and with or without a corner, creating a prayer cloth is sure to encourage peace.

PRAYER CLOTH

Make a prayer cloth for a permanently set up prayer table or for the center of the family food table, where it should be much smaller than the table itself, part of a centerpiece that will remain unstained by pasta sauce and chocolate ice cream.

For a teacher with a borrowed classroom, the cloth is light and easy to carry to class each week. It will give students a sense of continuity, plus pride in their creative contribution.

PRAYER CLOTHS

Materials

Unbleached muslin or white cloth larger than the prayer table on which it will go, with at least a four-inch extension on all sides

Magic markers, paper, pencils, and scissors

Optional: Sewing needle, thread, and pins

Sewing machine and/or embroidery needles, embroidery threads or yarns

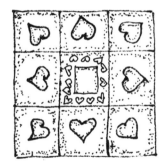

Preparation

Count the number of people who will contribute to the prayer cloth and divide it so that everyone will have a section. Rule out horizontal and vertical lines to form squares, or draw circles around plates, or form irregular patchwork sections. Don't worry if there are extra spaces; those who finish quickly can work on these. The important thing is to have at least one for everyone. For a large group, have another project going so small groups can take turns doing their sections.

Talk about why it is important to pray: We give a little of our time and attention to God, who gives us everything. We put aside busy thoughts to make room in our minds and hearts for God and the wonderful gifts God wants to give us: peace, love, joy, light, forgiveness, compassion, kindness, increased life, healing, and happiness—the expansion of all our talents and gifts.

Invite your group to work together to create a prayer cloth. Assign, or have each person choose, a section in which each will draw a symbol of a treasure that prayer brings.

Some popular symbols are: dove or peace sign; heart; sun; treasure box; jeweled cross; clasped hands; lamb; rainbow for harmony and hope; flowers for joy; sun or candle as a sign of God's presence to us; treasure or jewel box for all the gifts prayer brings.

If a glass table is available, place a lamp underneath so that the cloth can be placed over paper drawings and traced.

Doing the Craft

Choose the symbol you want to do. Draw it first on the paper with pencil, then on the cloth with markers. Try out different symbols and different ways of drawing them to see which you like best. Outline your choice with darker marker lines.

Those who finish early begin drawing on the cloth with markers. By placing your paper drawing under the cloth, you will have a guide for your cloth drawing. If the cloth is too heavy to see through, cut out parts of the drawing and trace around them. As drawings develop, help people choose ideas that differ from what other people do to avoid too much repetition (a little is okay).

Fill in the drawings with colored markers.

Hem the prayer cloth by hand or with the help of a machine and place it on the prayer table.

Variations

Embroider symbols with embroidery threads or yarns. Or use some of the techniques in "Cloth Arts" in the Introduction: satin stitch setting on a sewing machine, appliqué, hand hemming, etc.

Have people write their names or draw/cut out a figure to represent themselves for each space or for a border. Or represent each person by a heart; see Chapter 7 on banners.

Fasting

Fasting is similar to prayer; you give up a little of something material, rather than a bit of time, and receive so much more in return. Eating less doesn't hurt most people unless someone has an eating disorder and needs special help. The rest of us, who tend to indulge food cravings most of the year, benefit from consuming smaller quantities of rich foods and substituting foods that are high in nutrition.

Mardi Gras in the old days meant farewell to fat and rich foods for forty days. Today, it may also mean good-bye to extra fat on you! For spirituality, for health, and for added bonuses, the best "good-bye" includes refined sugar and flour in all forms, soda (use seltzer and fruit juice) cookies, cake and candy (have fruit and honey deserts), ice cream, and other nonessential treats.

Instead of encouraging indulgent eating, serve more vegetables and satisfy the body's need for protein with combinations of beans/lentils and whole grains, nuts, and dairy products. Use meats in smaller quantities in dishes that stretch them, such as pastas, ratatouilles, stews, and casseroles.

INTELLIGENT EATING

Center on intelligent eating. Fewer empty calories and more vegies and whole grains help both body and spirit. Food cravings lessen when the body receives the vitamins, minerals, and trace elements it needs.

For young people especially, fasting should be giving up what is less good for the body, not what is healthy and needed. Children often smile when a teacher says, "No fasting from vegetables—try skipping candy, cake, and sugary sodas."

Children need good nutrition in order to grow, but they will learn much from fasting (less food) and sometimes abstinence (no meat). And hard as it is, giving up sugary things that do them no good will help them to better health of body, mind, and spirit.

Granted, it's not easy for children to give up sweets; however, they are usually happy to know that Sundays do not count as fast days! Give them a good dessert then, and perhaps they can survive through the other six days. If that's too hard, there are hot cross buns, pretzels, and oatmeal cookies, depending on how desperate you think the situation is. Fasting should, after all, be voluntary, and Lent should be a time of happy growth.

It helps to know that fasting is physically as well as spiritually healthy when done sensibly. Some health experts advise adults to fast once a week, at least on fruits and vegetables, possibly on water and juices if the doctor says okay. Lent is a good time to start.

"It might be helpful to see a discipline like fasting as something we do for our bodies, rather than against our bodies... we can transfer our new healthy respect for the body to a respect for everybody: for all who are hungry in this world."
– Gertrud M. Nelson

TV FASTING

It's enriching to fast from other enjoyments as well. Limit TV time; certainly avoid programs that contain violence, vile language, and sexual immorality. Instead, do creative things; prepare for Easter with crafts. Develop conversation skills with family members and friends.

For good spiritual nutrition become more comfortable with silence, spiritual reading, and prayer; food fasting will be easier. A line from a psalm says, "Taste and see that the Lord is sweet." When the goodness, the joy of the spirit fills your awareness, craving for food is far less intense.

To further growth in faith, make decorative love menus and Lenten meal prayer sheets. This will help to keep the focus on spiritual nourishment and the inner treasures you gather as you give up superficial excess.

THE ABUNDANT LEVEL

In the 1970s the Liberty Eatery and Antique Emporium in Whitehall, New York, was in operation as a restaurant. The food menu, listing baked ham, chicken, and luscious desserts, was painted on an old wooden ironing board. Before showing this to guests, however, the owner brought out a different menu, also painted on an antique board.

This menu listed spiritual things served in the eatery: the Golden Rule; the "Big Ten" (commandments); peace and joy; love; courtesy and kindness. Add forgiveness, friendship, family love, compassion, and generosity and you have ideas for a Lenten feast, not on the material level of scarcity but on God's level of abundance.

On God's level, there are no limits, there is always more. During Lent, it's good to eat less physical food so that those in need have their share of a limited supply. On the spiritual level, however, the more you give away, the more you have, the more others have, the more there is. Serve up a spiritual menu and everyone will be better nourished with the things that count.

A SPIRITUAL MENU

As a Lenten craft, create a spiritual menu that lists the good things from God's abundant level that you want to dish up during Lent. You may not have access to an antique wooden ironing board, but you can easily rustle up some ordinary drawing or construction paper, paper plates, or even paper placemats, available in restaurant supply houses.

Spiritual Menu

Write a spiritual menu or meal prayer in the lines below.

©Jeanne Heiberg 1996.

Materials

White paper, paper plates, or placemats
Magic markers and/or crayons, tempera paints, or watercolor
Optional: Magazines, newspapers, scissors, glue
Plastic wrap or acetate cut to size of menu

Preparation

Discuss the reasons for a Lenten fast, the valuable things to be gained (see the chapter on resolutions and sacrifices and the Introduction).

List spiritual treasures you would like to serve up during Lent, such as those in "The Abundant Level," above. Think of all the good things that you can give away and have more of at the same time: love, forgiveness, happiness, etc. Brainstorm to generate a long list so that people will have good ideas to choose from.

Doing the Craft

Write out a menu with markers/crayons or paste on cut-out letters or words from magazines/newspapers. Decorate the menu with appropriate symbols or pictures drawn with markers/crayons or cut out and pasted into a collage.

Variations

Work on a piece of wood with any of the above materials, or with tempera, acrylic, or oil paints.

Translate this project into cloth, using ideas and directions from "Cloth Arts" in the Introduction.

Draw your menu on an actual plate from a craft house that supplies the plate and paints, then laminates it for you, for a permanent work of art.

Make a food chart of healthy, inexpensive foods that will enable you to eat less for Lent yet be well nourished. Illustrate it with drawings of the foods (vegetables are wonderful to draw; they have great shapes) or cut them out of magazines to make a collage.

SPIRITUAL MENU

MEAL PRAYERS

Make fasting meals a spiritual feast. Begin with special meal prayers hand-decorated by family members. In a class, have the children decorate them, then send them home to help families live Lent in a prayerful way.

A MEAL PRAYER FOR LENT

*Loving God, creator, as you
renew the earth in spring, so you
also renew us during Lent. Help us
to live it fully, willingly rooting
out lesser things to make room for
things of greater value that will last
forever and never let us down.*

*May we listen to you in prayer
with greater attention and grow
wiser, eat simpler food and grow
healthier, give of our things and
ourselves to others and grow happier
so that seeds of your life and love
may take root in us and flourish.*

*Bless this meal and bless our
sharing so that inner gardens of
your peace, love, and joy may grow
in us, in Jesus, our brother, through
whom we pray and are renewed.
Amen.*

*Help the seeds planted around this prayer to grow leaves and flowers as a sign
of the inner gardens God grows in our minds and hearts as we live a good Lent.
Use crayons/markers or cut and paste from colored paper.*

© Jeanne Heiberg 1996

Make copies of the prayers in this book for children to add onto with markers/crayons, or compose and design your own. Or ask children to write their own meal prayers, with illustration. Use the plate drawing as inspiration or as a pattern, blowing it up to meet your needs.

Almsgiving

Fasting provides extra monies from the food and entertainment budget which can be donated to groups that feed and help the hungry, poor, sick, and homeless.

See where else such funds can be supplemented from the personal and family budget. Brainstorm as a family, class, or group to see how money can be raised for such organizations as Bread for the World, Crop, or groups sponsored by your church.

Put some of your time, as well as your money, at the service of others. Children may be willing to help more in the family to earn alms. Parents may find a service in the community to give their children one of the most precious gifts: a good example.

The scarce/abundant levels apply to almsgiving as well as fasting. "Less is more" when you limit the material and feast on the spiritual. When you give away what you are not using, and even a little more, you end up with less on the limited level of the material world, but you enter further into the great, unlimited abundance of God's world, where the real treasures are.

Sometimes this even feeds back into the material level. The story is told of a businessman who failed in enterprises, one after another, until he was well on in years. Then he had a religious conversion and began to tithe, giving up ten percent of his income to God's work. His next enterprise was a huge success; his special chicken recipe made millions of dollars for Colonel Sanders.

Of course, not everyone who tithes is rewarded so well financially, but everyone reaps inner riches. Scripture and the experience of most churches also assure that the basic needs of tithers will always be met.

It is good for children to learn this early. They may not have much to give, but if it is only a dollar, a quarter, even a nickel, it matters. God sees the heart. They need to know that God also uses the care, the generosity, and the love behind the giving of alms to heal and help the needy of the world.

A young boy gave Jesus a small gift of bread and fish, very likely all

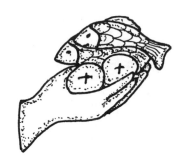

he had for his lunch. Jesus multiplied that gift to feed a multitude. God is not limited and can multiply even the smallest of gifts, given with love from the heart.

Whether children have offerings that are small or large, each has some gift that will enable them to express God's love by helping others.

To encourage children in this idea, show them how to make a decorated mite box to receive their own alms and the offerings of a family or class during Lent. This will help them remember the gospel woman noticed by Jesus for her generosity. Giving her all, she entered into God's level, the level of abundance, to shine forever as a symbol of giving.

MITE (OR ALMS) BOX

There is a choice in the size of the mite box: a large one for the family or class, or small, individual ones for each person. Any box will do: a shoe or cereal box, a used gift box, one made of corrugated cardboard, or one previously used for soap powder, tissue, or any other dry product. Avoid boxes that have contained messy materials (like pizza, prunes, or raisins).

Materials
    A small box for each person, or a large box for a group
    Scissors, glue sticks, white glue
    Papers, preferably in muted, near-to-neutral colors: construction,
        typing, color swatches from magazines, art tissue, sandpaper,
        paper bags, and other wrappers
    Optional: Brushes, water, plastic cups, and paper towels
            Cotton batting, burlap, and other cloth swatches in
                interesting textures, muted colors
            Small quantities of dried kitchen foods with varying
                textures: rice, tea, coffee, popcorn kernels, lentils, split
                peas, beans, sugar, salt
            Newspapers and/or a wide box or plastic sheet

Preparation
    For larger groups, have kitchen texture foods in plastic baggies, one set to every four people.
    For smaller children, precut a hole in the top of the box so that money can be pushed through.

Choice of Materials and Motivation

Explain the meaning behind Lenten almsgiving. Tell the story of the widow's mite. Ask people to express the meaning of almsgiving in their mite box design. They might want to depict the widow and her mite, or the boy offering Jesus his loaves and fishes. They may want to say it simply with symbols or colors and shapes. Earth colors are appropriate to Lent: browns, beiges, bricks, rusts, ochres, plus black, gray, and white. Many of these colors can be found in magazine swatches.

Photos and words found in magazines may also be used to show needs in the world that the mite box will help. Newspapers offer information about what is happening closest to the time the project takes place; black-and-white is appropriate for Lent. Combine it with grays and muted colors from other sources.

Another kind of box may develop the idea of abundance. Use photos of the greens and flowers of spring or the plenty of vegetables for the table. Establish them as symbols of the spiritual riches that come from using less in order to share more with others.

While keeping faith building to the fore, you can also offer materials of different textures to help three- to six-year-old minds prepare for reading. Help them to see and use words for different qualities: rough, smooth, fine, course, hard, soft, etc. Encourage all ages to use shapes that are big, medium, and small so that their collage will have nice contrasts. Point out the richness of the world that God has given them to explore.

To build faith further, point out that just as there are so many kinds of textures, shapes, and colors, there are also so many different kinds of people in the world, and God loves ALL of them, each and every one, very much.

Doing the Craft

Cover the box according to one of the collage methods explained in the "Paper Crafts" or "Painting" sections of the Introduction.

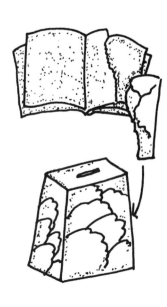

Variations

Use different textures from kitchen foods in your collage with color swatches or by themselves. Coat the place where you want them to stick by brushing on white glue, then sprinkle on finer textures such as salt, tea, or coffee. Place larger things, like beans, one at a time by hand.

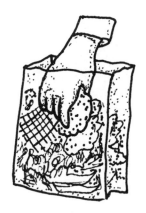

Kitchen materials, along with those from the workbench (sandpaper, sawdust, steel wool, etc.) and sewing-basket supplies will expand even further the range and excitement of the project. They are ways of saying that everything you do, everything you have, including your talents and gifts and the very different gifts of your neighbor, can be used to serve God.

Some may object that food should not be used for art since people need it to eat. A mite box covering, however, uses very little, and the craft helps people to see visual beauty in the gifts of the earth as it develops imagination and creativity.

When used to make a mite box special, food materials help to build faith and a concern for the needs of others. This is not a waste; the food provides nourishment for heart, mind, and spirit.

Follow-up Activity

Keep the box in a prominent place where people gather. Ask them to give something of what they earn as allowance or for work, and all that they save from simpler Lenten living. Plan inexpensive meals using plant proteins instead of meat, as suggested in "Fasting." Put the money saved in the mite box.

Prayer, Fasting, and Almsgiving Prayers

In the blessing that follows, change the wording to suit your family, class, or group. There may be specific things you want to add or eliminate in the first line. The third line should contain things that people in your group are going to give up so that others will be helped. If "part of my allowance" or "money from a bake sale" is what will go into the box, that is what your prayer should say.

You may want to do the blessing alone right after the box is finished or at a family meal or during a class. It can also be part of the longer prayer, with scripture, that follows. Shorten or eliminate readings for younger children; use the elements that are best for you and your people.

BLESSING OF A MITE BOX

Lord, you have blessed us with good things: food, clothing, a home, kind people, and your love surrounding us. We know there are others in the world with less, who suffer needs; we want to be your partners in helping them. This Lent, we pledge ourselves to _____ (eat a little less, have simpler meals, give up sweets, etc.—*fill in here what you and your people decide to do*) so that your blessings may extend to all who are open to your love.

Bless this mite box and the offerings it will receive. May our sacrifice of such a little be multiplied in blessings for those helped. May we feel the peace and joy of those who act in Jesus, through whom we pray and give. Amen.

SCRIPTURE-BASED PRAYER FOR ALMSGIVING

OPENING SONG: "Love Round," Servant Music, or "They Who Do Justice," *Today's Missal*

OPENING PRAYER: Lord, we gather in the name of Jesus, your son, who came to teach us how to live as your people. Open our minds and hearts to your word so that we may feast on spiritual treasures as we forgo some of our temporal time and goods. This Lent, help us to let go of some lesser and temporary things to reap joys that are everlasting. Amen.

OPTIONAL READINGS: Psalm 41:1-4 or Tobit 4:5-11; 1 John 3:17-19

GOSPEL READING: Mark 12:41-44 or Luke 12:32-34

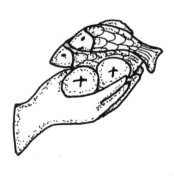

SONG: "Seek Ye First" or "Whatsoever You Do," *Today's Missal,* or "A Circle of Love" or "Welcome to the Kingdom" from *Rise Up and Sing,* Oregon Catholic Press

LITANY PRAYER: God calls us to be kind and to share our gifts with others who have need of them. The response to these prayers will be: LORD, HEAR OUR PRAYER.

That we may learn to live on God's abundant level of peace and generous love: RESPONSE.

That we may trust in God to meet our needs, and be willing to let go of our excess, and a little more: RESPONSE.

That we may be generous in our almsgiving to help the poor, sick, hungry, and homeless, and that God would bless them and take care of them: RESPONSE.

That we may see the needs of those around us and do what we can to help them: RESPONSE.

That we may always know we are loved by God, and grow in God's life this Lent: RESPONSE.

Lord, hear the prayers that we speak and those we hold in our hearts. Teach us to trust you for our own needs and to reap the peace and joy of giving to others. Amen.

"Perhaps our attitude to God is not visible, but we can test it in our behavior to our neighbor."
– Anthony Bloom

THE BLESSING OF THE MITE BOX: *Gather the group around the box and ask them to extend one hand over it as you pray the blessing (printed above).*

CLOSING SONG: "They Who Do Justice" or "They Who See Light" or "The Cry of the Poor," *Today's Missal,* or "Building the Kingdom," from *Hi God 4,* Oregon Catholic Press

PRAYER AND FASTING PRAYER FOR LENT

A loaf of whole-grain bread, or a plate of matzo with enough for a piece for each, and grape juice (or wine with discretion for adults) in small plastic cups on a tray are needed for part of this prayer.

OPENING SONG: "Throughout This Forty Days" or "The Quiet Song" by Nelly Brown Bunk

GOSPEL READING: Matthew 4:1-4, 11

Read the spiritual menu that people in your group have composed.

EATING AND DRINKING RITUAL: *(Pass bread/matzo so that all can break off a piece, then pass grape juice [or wine]. Ask them to hold up their bread as you pray:)*

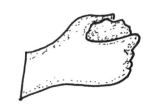

Lord, as we give up some of our food in fasting, feed us with bread for the spirit, your word and your love. Help us to spring-clean away unnecessary clutter in our minds and hearts to be more ready for the peace and love you want to give us.

(Invite all to eat their bread. Ask them to hold up their grape juice as you pray:)

Lord, as we give up some of our treats and unnecessary sweets in fasting, satisfy our thirst for enjoyment with the sweetness that comes from you in prayer. Teach us to listen to your voice in our inner mind and heart so that we will grow closer to you, to your Holy Spirit, and to Jesus, your son, in whom we pray. Amen.

(Invite all to drink their grape juice.)

CLOSING SONG: "The Quiet Song" (Nelly Brown Bunk) or "Peace Is Flowing Like a River" (Servant Music/*Today's Missal*)

CHAPTER 4

The Victorious Cross

W hat better time to make crosses than during Lent? The cross, not the crucifix, is the standard of Christianity, the central symbol of Christian faith.

History of the Cross

Crosses were not used that often in the very early church. Christians undergoing persecutions needed to keep their identity secret. This was best done by using very simple signs, such as a fish, from Greek initials referring to Christ which formed the Greek word for "fish." They also used a monogram for Christ: Chi, the Greek *X*, superimposed over a Rho, the Greek *P*, so that a cross was also formed.

In the catacombs, a cross or Chi-Rho was often at the center of vines and vine leaves to remind Christians of their oneness in Christ, according to his words, "I am the vine, you are the branches." At first glance, it might appear to be a decorative motif rather than a symbolic one endangering the lives of the faithful.

From these earliest days until well into the sixth century and beyond, only crosses were made to remind the faithful of what Christ had done for them. People who lived under Roman rule had seen actual crucifixions and thought them too awful to depict artistically. They were also intimately acquainted with the suffering side of the cross through the persecutions. Christians of that time needed to remember that Jesus' death had ended in resurrection.

Chi-Rho Cross and Vine

Jeweled Cross

Greek Letters say:
ICXC: Initials for
Jesus Christ
NIKA: Is Victorious
(spelled out)

Easter Cross

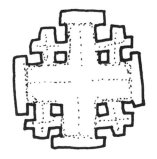

Jerusalem Cross

The persecutions ended after the emperor Constantine had a vision of a cross leading him to victory. Crosses began to be made and used more extensively. Artisans still emphasized the victory of the cross and fashioned them as symbols of heaven, covered with silver, gold, and precious jewels.

This is why the Roman Catholic Church until recently (sometimes still) followed the custom of veiling crosses with purple cloth during the weeks preceding Easter. Although it is the time of year when the focus is most on Christ's redeeming work on the cross, early works embodied so much of the resurrection and of heaven in their design that they were considered inappropriate for viewing during Lent. Covering these beautiful works of art, then unveiling them at Easter became a dramatic visual statement of Jesus' victory over sin and death.

A few centuries later, as Christians began to need a reminder of Christ's suffering and their own need to carry their cross, the figure of Jesus was gradually added.

In a canon passed by the Council of Trullo, A.D. 692, the practice of adding a lamb to the top of the cross is indicated. It is decreed that, in the future, "the figure in human form of the Lamb who taketh away the sin of the world be exhibited in images, instead of the ancient lamb, so that all may understand by means of it the depths of the humiliation of the Word of God, and that we may recall to our memory his conversation in the flesh, his passion and salutary death, and his redemption...."

In the eighth century, Saint John of Damascus defended the use of religious symbols, including the cross and other icons of faith. He pointed out many references to the cross in scripture, citing both testaments. He saw a need for respect and veneration toward even the symbols associated with God and Jesus and emphasized their value to Christians as visible reminders of invisible beliefs.

An iconoclastic controversy in the eighth and ninth centuries tried to do away with all Christian symbols and representations, so that believers were deprived of any public symbols of faith. Because St. John of Damascus believed they were windows on heaven, reminders of God, Jesus, and faith, icons and crosses were restored to churches.

As figures of Jesus began to be added to these early crosses, they were highly symbolic and abstract, not at all realistic. Most of the time they were still adorned with bright colors, silver, gold, and jewels.

Gradually images became more realistic, showing a more human, suffering Jesus. A famous thirteenth-century cross by the Italian artist Cimabue shows a stylized figure of Jesus painted on the cross that for the first time had emotion and suffering on his face. Slightly more realistic frescoes by Giotto followed, with grief obvious in the faces and postures of Jesus, his mother Mary, and others, in a pietà. Even the swooping angels wring their hands and show grief.

From that time on, more emotion, feeling, and realism developed in the art form we now call the crucifix. Although many help us to empathize with Jesus and understand his love, the danger is that we lose sight of the cross as a sign of both the death and resurrection, the suffering and victory of Jesus. While a wealth of wonderful art has been created by skillful and great artists inspired by the crucifix, it is still the cross that remains the symbolic norm for the Christian faith.

Making crosses in various forms is an ideal way to focus on ideas pertaining to the heart of Christian faith and how it relates to present situations. Themes for discussion are included here to encourage working with the hands and mind at the same time for the most effective faith-building process. Adapt these ideas to your people, draw on your own experiences as well, look at what is interesting to them and happening to them. Life offers many opportunities for discussions of the cross, the difficulties, and how God wants to help us through them.

DISCUSSION THEMES

Verticals and Horizontals

The cross is made up of two lines or bars: one horizontal, one vertical. Some say the vertical line represents our link, our dialogue, our relationship with God, while the horizontal bar represents our relationship with the people, the life, the world around us. When you try to keep both relationships going well, a creative tension is produced that is the cross. It isn't always easy, but it is, ultimately, the only way to be happy.

What is important to you in each of these areas of relationship? What is most difficult? What is most joyful?

During Lent, how can you deepen loving relationship with God? With others?

What happens when these two areas of life are out of balance, when either one is neglected? What are the rewards for keeping them in balance?

Precursors of Crucifix:

Lamb under Cross

Lamb on Cross

Peace Cross

Cross over World
Ascension Cross

Easter New Life Cross

Maltese Cross

Celtic Cross

Take Up Your Cross

Discuss Jesus' words: "Unless you take up your cross and follow me, you cannot be my disciple." What crosses do you encounter in everyday life as you do your best as a family member, friend, student, worker, and neighbor? Why is it sometimes difficult to share, give love, and put forth your best effort?

Discuss what Lenten practices would best help you to grow in generosity, discipline, and love during Lent. Think of time-honored Lenten ways of embracing the cross: prayer, fasting, and almsgiving; making resolutions and sacrifices; becoming just a little more like the seed falling into the ground, dying to itself, to rise with increased life a hundredfold in love and service. Other chapters provide material to help you reflect on these questions.

How can making sacrifices during Lent help you to overcome self-centeredness, to see God, rather than yourself, as the center of the universe? How can giving up small things prepare you for greater disciplines and difficulties that life may bring you in the future?

What needs in your family, community, church and world are greater than your own need for comfort, enjoyment, and entertainment? What could you give up without injury to your health, education, work, and good relationships with others? What could you do and give to meet the real needs of others?

TWIG AND BRANCH CROSSES

The most simple and appropriate cross to make for Lent is also the easiest. The materials are no further away than the nearest backyard, park, or woods where twigs and branches can be found. Gather some, two for each person who will make a cross, or ask others to do the gathering. Dig up old string from your kitchen cupboards or buy some twine, and you are all set.

Materials

Twigs or branches one-quarter- to three-quarter-inch thick, five to twelve inches long

Twine, string or yarn—brown, beige or white

Scissors

Optional: Small saw to make twigs shorter

Glue or glue gun

Preparation

Introduce cross-making as a reminder of how much Jesus loves you, what he gives to you, and the Lenten resolutions you can do for God, others, and yourself.

Making the Crosses

Tie together two twigs at right angles. Place the string over the two branches in one direction, then in another, to form an X across the front. Tie firmly in back.

Twig Cross

If the sticks wobble, weave the string over and under a few times, clockwise, then wind around one twig to go counterclockwise, over the branches the previous string went under and under where it went over. You may also hold it with a dab of glue or glue stick. Tie the string, then before cutting, form a loop for hanging or use a small eye hook toward the top.

Variations

1. Use small, squared lengths of wood for the cross. Mark the front of the vertical piece and the back of the horizontal piece with the width of the other piece where it will cross. With a penknife, whittle halfway down into each so that one can be inserted into the other. Place glue in the recesses, join together, and leave until the wood dries. Use a small eye hook on the back for hanging.

2. Make large crosses several feet high and wide out of thicker branches, up to two inches in diameter. In addition to twine or rope, drive a nail from the back that will pierce both branches at the center, without going through to the front of the cross.

CRAFT-PICK CROSSES

← tagboard
← craft pick

Craft-pick Cross

Materials

Twenty-four craft picks* for each cross
Tagboard, light cardboard, or heavy paper
White glue or glue gun and scissors
Shiny gold or silver origami (or wrapping) paper
Optional: Other colored papers, metallic gold paper twist, small round mirrors or flat glass "jewels" one-half inch in diameter, or sequins, small beads, buttons, felt pieces, or small jewel-like stickers
Markers and/or paint, tempera, or acrylic

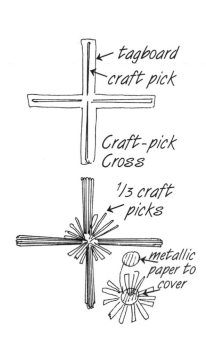

1/3 craft picks

← metallic paper to cover

* Craft picks are slightly larger than toothpicks, wider at one end, tapering almost to a point at the other. Toothpicks may be used in a pinch, but the cross will be smaller.

Doing the Craft

On a piece of tagboard (or other), place four toothpicks in a cross form, points to the center, leaving open a three-eighth-inch space at the center. Place two more craft picks on either side of (and close to) the first pieces, pointing to the center. Keep the space they form at the tips even.

Trace around the cross you have formed on the tagboard. Remove the picks and cut out the cross, making it slightly smaller, just inside the lines at the sides, and one-quarter inch smaller at the ends.

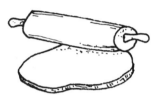

Smooth glue on one arm of the cross and replace the picks. To hold well, also dab a little glue on the sides of each piece where they fit together. Repeat with all four arms.

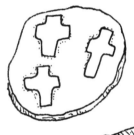

Break the remaining craft picks into one-inch pieces and place in a circle at the center of the cross, so that they radiate out from the center like the rays of a sun. Glue these in place.

Place a one-half-inch circle of shiny paper, or other jewel-like circle, over the center of the "sun" at the center of the cross.

This will make a beautiful cross, but you can also add more "jewels" and colors.

To finish, glue a loop of string in back (top) for hanging; a glue gun works well. A large needle and thread passed through the cardboard will also make a sturdy hanger.

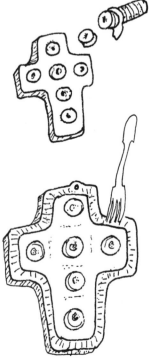

COOKIE CROSSES

Lent is not the time to eat these sugar crosses, and it may be a sacrifice to wait until Easter, but it is worth it. You may even want to keep them to look at permanently.

Materials

A batch of cookie dough made from your favorite sugar cookie recipe, or biscuit or ready-to-bake dough from the supermarket

Multicolor Life Savers

Rolling pins, round glasses or bottles, or thick wood dowels

Table knives and toothpicks

Cookie sheets and aluminum foil

Doing the Craft

Roll out the dough to a one-quarter-inch thick large "blanket." From this, cut out cross shapes with a knife or toothpick. Use a toothpick, fork prongs, or a skewer to add borders, decorative lines, etc. Work in Lifesavers as "jewels" to decorate a glorious cross. With a toothpick, make a hole at one end and place a small piece of aluminum foil in it to keep it open.

Place the cross on an aluminum foil-covered cookie sheet. Bake at 350 degrees until Lifesavers melt and dough is done. Remove from oven, take crosses off with a spatula, and allow to cool.

Put string through the hole at the top for hanging.

GLORIOUS PAPER CROSSES

Making glorious paper crosses can be as simple or complex as you wish, ranging from use of crayons or markers to making a collage from construction paper, art tissue, magazine swatches, or photos.

Easter Cross

Materials

    White drawing or construction paper, colored construction paper,
        OR colored art tissue, OR color swatches from magazines
    Shiny metallic origami or wrapping papers
    Glue or glue stick
    Scissors
    Markers and crayons
    Pencils
    Optional: Tagboard or light cardboard
               Hole punch
               Yarn or string
               Prepared outline of cross copies, one for each person

Resurrection Cross

Preparation

Have your choice of materials ready, plus prepared copies you want to use: copies of crosses from this book or other sources, blown up to the size you need, OR make your own designs, OR recruit an artistic friend to make them. Be sure to have white paper and pencils, and encourage people to do their own designs.

Motivation

Discuss the cross as a symbol of Christian faith, expressing both the death and resurrection of Jesus. Show different forms and shapes the cross can take.

Discuss ways of expressing the resurrection, the victory of Jesus, in a cross: gold, jewels, vine and branches, bright colors, suns, and other symbols of life, love, or Easter. Discuss the early Christian use of the vine and branches and the cross.

Doing the Craft

Choose or design the shape of your cross and outline it in pencil or marker on a background paper. Cut out interesting shapes and colors from other papers and place them on the background to form your cross and its symbols/decorations, or do the same with crayons, markers, or paint.

Variations

Do something interesting with the background shape: fill it in with rays, vine branches with leaves, or baptismal or growing symbols; OR put in the corners: symbols of the four seasons or the four directions (north, east, south, west) to show the universality of Jesus' death and resurrection; it is for all times, all peoples, the whole world.

Instead of filling in the four corners, cut out your cross and back it with tagboard or light cardboard. Punch a hole in the top and hang with yarn.

Draw your cross on foamcore, cut it out with an X-acto or foamcore knife, decorate, and hang.

Use photos cut out from magazines to show the sufferings in the world, the cross in the world now.

Make a large cross of paper, cardboard, foamcore, or cloth. Have people prepare what will go on it, and bring it up to attach during a time of prayer. The additions may be: bright paper "jewels," or vine and branches, or photos and drawings of suffering in the world that the group wants to help heal through prayer and almsgiving.

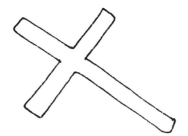

Way of the Cross

GLORIOUS CLOTH CROSSES

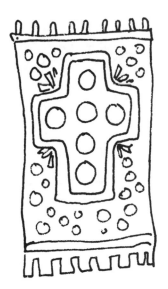

Materials

    Plain paper and pencils to form patterns

    Felt background shapes, nine by twelve inches, for each person to
        make a cross, or larger pieces in your choice of size

    Felt pieces or scraps in many bright colors

    Scissors, glue, pins, needle and thread

    Wood dowel and string or yarn

See "Cloth Arts" for other materials for a background piece on which to assemble the crosses into one large banner or quilt.

Doing the Craft

Follow the steps in "Glorious Paper Crosses" to achieve paper patterns in the design you want to do in cloth. Follow the instructions in "Cloth Arts" in the Introduction for your choice of methods and materials for banners with one large design. See Chapter 7 for ways to plan and assemble smaller, individually made pieces into a unified whole.

Prayers

CREATING A CROSS FOR PRAYER

Make a large hanging cross in your choice of materials. Prepare symbols to be brought up and attached during prayer. A wood or foam-core cross will allow the use of pushpins or thumbtacks; for paper or cardboard, use rolled up masking tape on the back, or glue sticks. With a cloth cross, use pins, Velcro, or the flannel-board effect of felt on felt. Felt wrapped around cardboard to form a cross makes a good flannel-board background for symbols to be easily attached. The symbols may be "jewels," the vine and branches, new life symbols, photos, or drawings.

To put photos or drawings on felt, paste sandpaper or felt on the backs. For older children, use pictures of problems and suffering in the world they want to help heal through prayer and almsgiving.

The ritual of building a cross may be seen as a wish to receive God's love, a willingness to share in the life of Jesus, and a readiness to

Calvary Cross

take a stand for Jesus in what is right, as he took a stand for you. This also means a readiness to trust in God through the difficulties of life, knowing that God will help you overcome them. Plan a theme appropriate to the age and needs of those who will participate.

Preparation

Have ready a prayer table with a bible, candles, and the basic cross on which symbols will be attached, plus symbols or pictures that people will bring up individually. You may also have a few representatives attach these. Prepare these in advance, according to directions in the previous crafts.

See the "Victorious Cross Prayer" in "Lenten Resolutions" for more ideas; also look at booklets and readings from your church. Expand the prayer and readings, or make them shorter, according to the age and needs of your group.

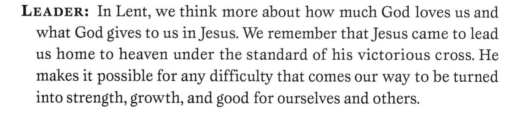

GLORIOUS CROSS PRAYER

Byzantium Cross

LEADER: In Lent, we think more about how much God loves us and what God gives to us in Jesus. We remember that Jesus came to lead us home to heaven under the standard of his victorious cross. He makes it possible for any difficulty that comes our way to be turned into strength, growth, and good for ourselves and others.

OPENING SONG: "Lift High the Cross," *Today's Missal*

OPENING PRAYER: Gentle, loving God, you help us through all our difficulties, turning them to joy when we turn to you. Under the victory cross of Jesus, you receive us as your children and guide us into ways of life forever. Help us this Lent to become stronger Christians, renewed in Jesus, in whom we pray. Amen.

READINGS: 1 Corinthians 1:18-25; Matthew 10:38-39; 16:24-27

COMMENTARY: Jesus carried his cross to bring all of us home safely into God's kingdom of peace and joy. Our crosses are little compared to that of Jesus, but through them he will help us to discover who we really are: God's children, brothers and sisters of Jesus. He was strong for us, and he will help each of us to be strong for God and for each other. In him we will discover our true self, made in our creator's image to be loving and good, peaceful, strong, and happy.

RITUAL ACTION: To celebrate the victorious cross that opens heaven's gates and gives everlasting life to all who live in God, we will create a (cross or banner) together. Spend some quiet time now thinking of how many times you have grown and discovered more of who you are, when you turned to God through difficulties and problems. Think also about when you might ask God's help so that you will experience this more often.

In thankfulness for the life we receive through Jesus and the cross, and as a prayer that God will help us turn difficulties into victories, bring up your part of the banner whenever you feel ready and add it to the whole.

(Play music and demonstrate how a part is to be added on by gluing, pinning, drawing, Velcro, etc.)

BLESSING OF THE CROSS/BANNER: Lord, you give us so many blessings through Jesus and his victorious cross. You teach us who we really are, your children, made in your own image and in the likeness of love itself.

Bless now this (cross or banner) we have assembled here, that it may become a sign of our readiness to take up our own cross and follow Jesus, knowing that your love will carry us through any hard places to strengthen us and bring us joy.

May all the crosses that we wear or place on our walls help to keep our focus on you and the abundant life you share with us in him through whom we pray, Jesus your son. Amen.

CLOSING SONG: "Take Up Your Cross," *Today's Missal*, Oregon Catholic Press

Egyptian T or Tau Cross (with or without loop on top)

CHAPTER 5

Desert Retreat: Sand and Cactus

Lent is the yearly retreat for Christians, the time to follow Jesus' example of going out into the desert to fast and pray and be close to God. Then, as after any good retreat, people bring back to their everyday world a wiser, more loving person, better able to solve the problems they contend with.

Everyone faces many problems in their everyday worlds of family, friends, work, school, and community, and together the human community contends with many world crises and disasters. In the desert, however, you are able to go to the heart of things and discover that there is only one problem, one solution.

JESUS IN THE DESERT

Jesus went into the desert at the beginning of his public ministry to fast, reflect, and pray, all the things people do in modified form during Lent. He dealt very personally with the one problem: separation from God.

The most extreme image of separation from God, the devil himself, appears to Jesus when he is physically weakened by fasting. Satan offers purely physical food, possessions, power, and pride in exchange for homage. Jesus refuses; he chooses instead the solution: unity with God and service to his brothers and sisters. Physically weakened, Jesus still remains spiritually strong; he will not let idols, ego, or anything come between his oneness with God.

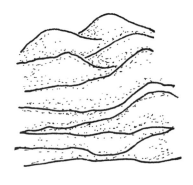

Lent is the time to follow Jesus into a symbolic desert to reflect on the problem yourself and make your choice for the solution to the one problem that every single person faces.

ONLY ONE PROBLEM

There are so many problems—in the world, in society, facing each person—that it is hard to believe that there is really only ONE PROBLEM, but it is true. The problem is this: we have become separated from God and from other people. God created us to be one with God, one with each other, one with creation, and one with the universe, all living in perfect love with God at our center. That is the way we were originally designed.

Along the way, the human race chose to be separated from God and from one another. God is love, life, light, peace, and joy, so the separation brought hate, death, illness, darkness, chaos, misery, and despair. This is the ONE PROBLEM.

ONLY ONE SOLUTION

The solution is not a what but a who, Jesus. God, who loves all, would not allow the separation to continue, would not allow the human race to remain sick, in misery, prey to evil, and headed for destruction. God sent Jesus to be the solution, to bring the whole human race back into unity with God, with other humans, and with all creation.

During the last supper, Jesus prayed: "Father, that they may be one in me, as I in thee, that they may be one in us."

The return to unity is achieved in Jesus, in entering into his death, resurrection, and new life in baptism. The unity grows as more people and more of each person come into the victory of Jesus in baptism. Evil is overcome, as it was in the story of Jesus in the desert. When the separation ends, the desert of the soul and mind becomes a flourishing garden.

A TIME OF HEALING

The oneness that is restored by God in baptism brings about healing, and each Lent renews it just when it is most needed.

Earlier, during the winter, people strengthen and comfort themselves against the winter cold by eating more and richer foods. To cheer themselves in the face of winter darkness, they go for more partying, socializing, sweets, and other indulgences.

Lent is the time to undo all that, to fast—to eat less but more nutritious food, geared to real needs. As fields are plowed up before the spring planting, the good Christian plows up the accumulation of old bad habits. It's time to get rid of winter's slush, weeds and debris, and colds and flus, and to make way for a spring sowing of spiritual growth and healing.

Native Americans also had times devoted to healings, with sandpainting to bring balance, unity, and harmony back into the minds of those who had fallen ill. Colored sands were used to make images perfect in symmetry, a prayer for perfect balance in one's inner life.

Since sand comes from the desert, a symbol of Lent, you can use it to express your willingness to go with Jesus into the desert, to live more austerely for a while, so that you are ready to receive God's healing. If you use it to create a mandala, it will also express your wish to enter into the one solution.

Several crafts using sand follow here to help inspire your Lenten spiritual trek into the desert, to help you leave behind lesser things for a wholehearted growth in God's love.

"Lent is a retreat in which we give up some things that are temporary and superficial, for things that are real, of immense value to us."
— Dave Protano, Catechist

Mandalas

A mandala is a work of art that is perfectly symmetrical, usually in circular form, though sometimes combining a square as well. The design radiates outward from a center, and that is the reason why it is considered a means of healing. When you are centered in God, when you are in tune with the presence of God at the very heart of your being, you are part of the one solution to the one problem. All other solutions in life radiate out from that, including healing.

When something disrupts the unity, blocks the flow of love, imbalances take place in the mind and the emotions, and these eventually affect the body as well. It may not be the fault of the one who falls sick, who bears the brunt of the problem, because the actions of each person reverberate throughout the whole of life. It is not part of the solution to judge or blame any one person, especially one who is sick, but rather to work toward centering oneself in God and uniting in peace, love, and joy with others.

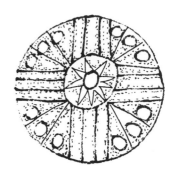

The circular shape of the mandala is sacred to the Native American because in a circle everyone is on the same level, equal before God, with none above or below, as on a ladder. The circle expresses oneness with your fellow human beings. Without a beginning or end, the circle also expresses eternity.

This makes the mandala a sign of, and a prayer for, the one solution. Its perfect, peaceful symmetry and its centeredness make it a symbol of heaven and also of prayer, our way to experience God and heaven now. By making the mandala and its meaning a focus for your awareness, it can help to restore you to centeredness in God, with healing of mind, heart, and often of body as well.

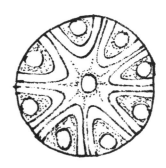

Materials

Colored sand from a craft store, or clean white sand plus a coloring agent: dry tempera paint, food coloring, or colored inks
White or tacky glue
Pencils
Transfer paper
A backing: sandpaper, emery paper, or poster board
Jars, bowls, or containers for mixing and holding the different colors, plus spoons, flat knives, brushes, and toothpicks for working with it
For Easy Method: Sandpaper backing and tempera or acrylic paint and brushes, water, paper towels

Preparing the Craft

Mix together sand and dry tempera in separate containers for each color. Begin with a drop or two of coloring for each one-quarter cup of sand, adding more until the color is deep enough for your satisfaction.

The traditional way to do sandpainting makes it an impermanent art, done for a time of prayer and healing, then discarded. This kind of sandpainting can be done in any flat-bottomed dish or on anything flat that will not be disturbed for a few days.

To give your sandpainting more longevity, try working it out on sandpaper or poster board with glue. You can use an easy method by simply painting on sandpaper or by building up layers of glue-sand,

glue-sand in a glue outline. Mixing the sand with glue into a paste and smoothing it on is another method.

Doing the Craft

Lightly sketch a mandala design in circular form, around a center. Think of how a snowflake radiates out, perfectly symmetrical on all sides, from a central point.

You might want to work a symmetrical cross into your mandala as another Lenten symbol. Draw shapes that feel right to you, remembering that you will fill them in with sand later.

Use a ruler to achieve symmetry, or design one section of a circle on tracing paper, then fold the paper into equal parts and repeat to fill the rest of the shape.

As you work, play straight lines against curved lines; repeat the kinds of lines and shapes you use to create rhythms; vary the size of the shapes you create for variety: smaller, medium, and bigger.

As you work, think of the lines and shapes you create as beautiful because they are radiating out from the one center, the one solution—the presence of God at the very center of your being. Make your work a creative conversation with God, a prayer.

When the design is completed, transfer it to the backing with transfer paper. You can also draw directly on the backing.

Easy Method for All Ages

Simply paint the design on a sandpaper or emery paper backing with tempera or acrylic paints.

For Children Eight to Nine Years and Up

Outline an area of the design with white or tacky glue; repeat in all the similar areas of the design. When they are dry, paint a layer of glue inside each raised glue area, then sprinkle in sand. Let these areas dry while you work on others, then return to repeat layers of glue and sand to build up an area. You may also use the tip of a knife and toothpicks to place the sand, using dry sand or sand dampened with food coloring, ink, or glue. The wet sand may be spread as a paste.

As you work, try to keep the surrounding areas clean. Use a vacuum with a hose attachment to pick up excess sand. Try not to let two wet outlines or areas touch. Use a hair dryer to speed drying time. Fill in all repeated shapes in different sections of the design with the same color.

Continue filling in shapes until the design is completed. If your circle is in a square, or will go into a square frame, think of the four corners, the background, as part of the design, even if you fill them in with one solid color.

Make the entire process part of your prayer, thinking of the different areas of your life and how you want them to be centered in the one solution: unity with God and with all God's children, united with Jesus in service and love.

If you want your work to last longer, spray it with a pastel fixative or hair spray in a well-ventilated place or outdoors.

OPTIONAL: Put the finished work in a plastic box frame, or between a heavier cardboard and a piece of glass with electrical tape or duct tape around the edges.

SAND ART IN A GLASS

This craft may be an individual or communal prayer. It may also be tied into a Lenten resolutions prayer.

Materials
A clear, uncolored glass, bowl, jar, or clear plastic cups (A clear vase or brandy-snifter works well for a communal craft. To allow a group to each keep their work, try baby-food jars, or the inexpensive clear plastic cups used for parties.)
Colored sands in jars, with a spoon for each color

Preparations
Tell people that sandpainting will remind them of Jesus' retreat in the desert and of what they will do in unity with Jesus on their own Lenten retreat. Any resolutions they make should be things that will later help them to grow in love and service.

If you fill the glass as part of a group-prayer meditation, ask people to come forward to put a layer of sand in the glass when they feel ready—when they have resolved to center themselves in God during Lent and have thought of one way they will do this. See the prayer at the end of this chapter.

Doing the Craft
Place different layers of colored sands in the glass with a spoon. Work for variety: thick layers against thin; layers that get thicker at the center, then taper off against growing thicknesses of layers above or below in a rhythmic flow.

Cactus Gardens

To express the desert theme of Lent, make a cactus garden. Churches sometimes use them in the sanctuary or main entryway to establish the desert theme of Lent.

Where holy-water fonts are used, they are emptied. Fonts at entrances serve as a reminder of baptism, the entryway into the Church, the people of God. At baptism, the celebrant signed the new member on the forehead and chest with a small cross movement of the thumb. This gesture said, "Now you belong to Christ, all of you, your mind and heart, and now you also belong to Christ's family, the Church. When believers repeat the sign of the cross with blessed water as they enter the church building, they are saying, "Yes, I still do want to belong." The original commitment, often made by others for the person, is ratified again by the believer. The belonging is recalled and rekindled.

Taking the water away during Lent reminds believers how much they need this water of life, this belonging to Christ. It is an invitation to go with Jesus into the desert with fasting and prayer, to search out anything that blocks the flow of that life-giving water in themselves, any inclinations to power, possessions, pride, or separating things that hold back life.

HARD QUESTIONS AND DIFFICULT TIMES

A desert cactus garden also reminds people to grapple with these questions during Lent. This may not be easy.

When God brought the chosen people, the Hebrews, out of slavery toward a promised land, they had to go through a desert and difficulties. They grumbled and complained. However, through the hard time in the desert, they grew into better people; they grew closer to God and one another.

Just like a desert, a difficult time often holds surprising beauty and hidden rewards when it brings us closer to God and neighbor. Empty holy-water fonts embody that message; cactus gardens can as well.

CACTUS PLANT HISTORY

Cactus plants originated only in the Americas. Eons ago, before even the dinosaurs, all the world was evenly warm and moist. Flowering plants, leafy trees, bushes, and vines grew in abundance; there were no cactus.

The climate changed; dry, arid areas grew. Some plants became cactus in order to survive. They lost leaves that evaporated too much moisture and grew thick stems with thick skins to hold and store water inside. They developed spines and prickles to fend off animals that would destroy them to get at that water.

CACTUS PLANTS AND PEOPLE

It's sometimes like that with people. We all have desert experiences, hard and difficult times. However, people who stay in the desert too long, who have too many hurts and hard things happen, sometimes become, in their hearts, a little like cactus. They develop tough outsides, hide their good inside, and grow prickles to keep people away. When we are hurt by someone, when they seem mean and prickly on the outside, it helps to know that they may have been too long in the desert; they need forgiveness, love, and prayers.

If someone has been mean to you or hurt you, you may have developed some prickles, a hard hide, and may be keeping good, life-giving things inside where no one can see them. It's time to learn more about how much God and Jesus love you, to get rid of some of the prickles, and to put out more flowers and friendly leaves and tendrils.

Here's how to make a cactus garden that will help you remember about cactus and people.

Materials
   Holders: for smaller cactus, a flat, low dish preferably of earthenware, or ceramic (You may also use a clay or plastic flower pot, the lower and wider the better.)
   Soil: a one-third each mixture of humus or potting soil, washed sand, and perlite (not vermiculite, which holds too much moisture) is ideal
   Rough rocks, gravel, or broken pottery pieces (rough and jagged, not smooth or rounded) for drainage

"We who have rationalized ourselves out of the symbolic world often forget how to allow simple objects or actions to become the container of the sacred. Incarnation is the flesh-taking of the sacred."

— Gertrud M. Nelson

Cactus: a selection with contrasting sizes and shapes. Try fishhook, pincushion, and different dwarf varieties.

Optional: Beautiful, interesting rocks and stones

Doing the Craft

Cover the bottom of the container with the rough stones and gravel, then add soil. Place the cactus, leaving enough space around each and between the garden and the edge of the bowl. Fill in with soil up to an inch from the rim. Place the rocks on top of the soil as part of the design.

Care: water well every other week during spring and summer; feed lightly and often. Give plants a rest during winter with less water, but don't let the roots dry out. Cactus need light, but not full sun for long periods of time.

Desert Sands Prayer

Materials

Everything listed for "Sand Art in a Glass," above

A prayer cloth or burlap

Bible, cross, and candles, and if possible, a cactus garden

A prayer table large enough to hold all this

Optional: A box or books to raise up the sand glass

          Music copies, cassette, taped music

Preparation

Make an attractive arrangement with the glass or bowl as the focus, possibly elevated by a box or books under the cloth. Place the different colored sands close to the glass so that those who are praying will see them and feel comfortable when they come up to place their layer of colored sand in the glass.

The advantage of creating the painting in a raised glass is that it can be seen by all; people can anticipate the ritual action and see it as it happens. Afterward, the sand painting remains as a symbol of the prayer.

OPENING SONG: "Hosea," *Today's Missal,* or "The Glory of These Forty Days," *With One Voice*

PRAYER: God our creator, thank you for your love. During this time of Lent, help us to trust you more and draw closer to Jesus so that you will be our center and we will put nothing before you and your people.

Give us caring minds to see where we may hurt others, and forgiving hearts to let go of our own hurts and make up with those who have caused them.

Help us to see that we all have different gifts with which to praise you and help one another. May we become more firmly centered in you and united in harmony and peace together as your family. Amen.

READING: Matthew 4:1-11 or John 4:13, 14

RITUAL ACTION: Ask people to contribute to a sandpainting as a sign of readiness to enter the Lenten desert with Jesus. When they feel ready, they may come to the prayer center, pick a color of their choice, and lay it wherever they wish in the glass in which the painting has already started. Play music and allow a time of reflective quiet until there has been enough time for everyone who wishes to contribute to the sandpainting.

BLESSING: Lord, our loving God, bless this painting of sand that we have just created together. May it help us to remember that our happiness and well-being flow from our unity with you and with one another. Each person present has gifts to give to our (family/community). By sharing and working together, we make something beautiful and good.

Bless each of us, Lord, to accept one another and to see your presence in ourselves and others. Help us to overcome any prickliness that comes from our own hurts in life. Help us to seek, instead, to help and not hurt those we deal with everyday: family, friends, and even strangers and passersby.

We may or may not have created a masterpiece of art in our sandpainting, but we ask you to bring to completion the masterpiece you are creating in all of us as we grow in you together. We ask this in him who came to bring us together and home to you, Jesus, your son. Amen.

CONTINUING THE PRAYER
THROUGH LENT

You may continue the sandpainting prayer during Lent by adding one more color during each week to symbolize different blessings of the season. Use prayers from the Lenten readings, or sing songs such as "Peace Is Flowing Like a River" or one of the songs at the back of this book. Colors you may use each week are:

1st: Beige, sand, and brown, for the desert retreat and for the inner plowing up that will be taking place, to open hearts further to new seeds of God's love.

2nd: Yellow and gold, for the transfiguration and the light of revelation Jesus came to bring; a reminder that Jesus makes us people of light and wants us to shine.

3rd: Blue, for baptism and the healing waters of life that will spring up in the desert areas of our minds and hearts to turn them into gardens, and for loyalty to Lenten resolutions.

4th: Blue and green, for the healing taking place in God's people and that they are called to bring to others in love and forgiveness.

5th: Greens and yellows, to express the new life that is sprouting during Lent, to burst forth at Easter.

6th: Purple and magenta, to express Jesus' kingship and his readiness to serve and sacrifice to help God's people.

Holy Thursday: Gold, golden brown, and yellow ochres, for many separate grains becoming the one lifegiving bread, God's people coming from separation into unity; plus deep red, for the wine of joy and unity in Christ.

Good Friday: Red, in honor of Christ's passion, and white, for the Lamb of God.

Holy Saturday: Quiet gray, light blue, and beige, for restful prayer and waiting.

Easter Sunday: Gold, pink, green, and yellow, all the colors of new life, sunrise, and happiness, to top off the sandpainting. If there is more room, continue to add light, bright colors during the Easter Season.

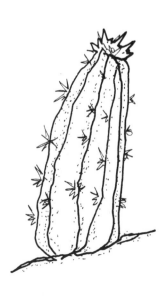

CHAPTER 6

Earth Arts: From Death to Life

There is a folk song that goes: *Lent comes in Spring, and Spring is pied with brightness, the fairest flowers, keen winds and sun and showers, their health do bring, to make Lent's chastened whiteness . . . arise, arise, arise and make a paradise!* This song refers to a major Lenten theme, derived from three sources:

1. The budding and blossoming of trees and flowers, the return of butterflies and birds, warm golden sunshine and longer days; in short, the human experience of nature's rebirth and renewal of life in spring.

2. The historic death of Jesus, and belief in his resurrection to an eternal, glorified life in God that he shares with God's people. This great hope for the human heart is symbolized and celebrated in nature's return to life, at least in the Northern Hemisphere, where the traditions grew.

3. The spiritual experience of baptismal death to sin and rebirth into Jesus, the new life he won, and the church he began. When the church lives as God intends, it creates a community of peace, justice, love, and joy, and from that flows the paradise the song celebrates. It happens more often in Lent, when people take time to reflect, fast, pray, give alms, and otherwise work to overcome all that separates them from God and their fellow humans. This results in a yearly fresh start in happiness.

The song is filled with the freshness and joy of spring, nature come back to life again after the darkness and cold of winter: carpets of green spreading over the earth; blossoms bursting from trees;

83

daffodils, tulips, butterflies, and birds all back again, joyfully welcoming winter-weary people.

The resurrection in nature of what, last autumn, appeared to die offers a hope that human life also is ongoing.

Most people dread death as the end of life. And they fear not only the big, final death but also the "little deaths" that cloud life now: pain, hurt, sickness, setbacks, resentment, loss, anger, and frustration of all kinds. The final big death, and even the little ones along the way, are dealt their own death blow by the resurrection of Jesus, foreshadowed in nature. All that humans fear and dread has been overcome by Jesus.

LIFE IS ONGOING

The natural spring, symbol of a spiritual reality, proclaims the good news: life is ongoing. In God there is no death, there is always life.

Of course something does die, even before the body finally dies at the end of life. Baptism is a death and a new life. What dies in baptism is only hardness of heart, selfish egoism, the part of the ego that separates itself from God and others. Jesus said, "Unless the seed falling into the ground die, itself remains alone; but if it die, it brings forth much fruit." The seed is like the "I" of St. Paul when he says, "I live now, not I, but Christ lives in me." He refers to the death of a false, selfish, unloving "I" that is not the true self created by God in God's own image. This true self was designed to be happy, living in peace, in joy, and in oneness with God and others.

The Lenten yearly retreat is a time to look within, to see what blocks to love have developed in one's life, and with God's help, to overcome them. Then the true Christ-self can emerge, grow, and bear fruit a hundredfold.

PREPARING FOR NEW LIFE

Lenten sacrifice and prayer can be seen as plowing up the inner earth and breaking up the hardness of heart caused by hurts, resentments, materialism—the clods of self interest that have accumulated. Lent is the farmer's time to plow up the earth, and it is also the time for Christians to plow up the inner fields, to make the inner life more receptive to the seeds of abundant life God wants to give. Jesus said, "I have come that you may have life, and have it more abundantly." With properly prepared inner soil, your soul-life becomes like a beautiful rich garden that is vivid with multicolored flowers and productive with nourishing fruits of the earth.

INNER AND OUTER GARDENS

As you teach children, it is best to show the good that comes when you plow up this "inner earth" of mind and heart. Emphasize the new life rather than what has to be sacrificed. However, you also want to be honest. Plowing up, rototilling, does involve work. You have to root out superficial things of passing value and pull out weeds that choke out the real life, God's life. However, when you consider what will be gained, such sacrifices as giving up TV and other treats, giving more time to prayer and scripture, and helping others more are next to nothing, easy, a joy.

Who does not want to be happier, to have more loving relationships, better health of mind and body, and increased peace, love, and joy? The self-esteem that comes from knowing that God loves you, the happiness that comes as you give and forgive, and the health and lightness of spirit that result from eating less and better food are unbeatable gifts. The abundant life of Jesus is sweet and wonderful, longed for once it is tasted. It gives happiness and strength not only to you but to those around you as well.

To keep the focus on life, there are external crafts and projects that will enrich both the inner soul-life and the external life of nature that comes within your scope. When the external activity and its inner meaning are seen as two sides of one coin, two happenings on different planes, both planes will feed and nourish each other. As you reflect and act together, they will provide you and your young people with motivation to grow in faith during the Lenten season.

"They who labor in the earth are the chosen people of God."
– Thomas Jefferson

PREPARING THE EARTH

The following projects involve preparing earth to receive seeds and celebrating their growth. The seeds become signs of the unseen new life planted in baptism and hidden in each Christian. Remind your young people often during the projects that God is continually giving us gifts of love, sowing them in our souls like a gardener planting seeds in a flower or vegetable bed or a farmer seeding a field.

Seeds grow better when the soil is prepared for it. God's life also takes root and sends up shoots when the mind and heart are ready. The external preparation of the earth, the creation of "super-soil" is a symbol of the inner preparation, the fasting, prayer, and almsgiving that are the norms for Lent.

These earth and seed projects can be done whether or not you have a garden or access to one; even cliff dwellers in city high-rise apartments can celebrate natural and spiritual new life in Lent with these crafts.

CARE OF THE PLANET

As is the garden,
so is the gardener.
— **Hebrew Proverb**

Preparing earth for seeds, and planting them are good reminders that humans are responsible for the continued health of the planet and for bringing back to health what has been sickened, polluted, and destroyed by shortsighted, irresponsible use. Caring for the earth that feeds all God's creatures is a newer dimension of Lenten preparation in our age.

Preparing Soil and Planting Seeds

Materials

    Small clay or plastic pots, or clear plastic glasses, or sprout/berry
        containers

    Potting soil

    Pebbles, gravel, or small stones

    Seeds: wheat, alfalfa (from the health food store), herbs, vegetable
        or flower

    Macramé or other cord, yarn, thin ribbon, paper ribbon, or paper
        cord (For hanging pots: eight strands from twenty-four to
        thirty inches long per small pot; longer for larger pots.)

    Newspaper or plastic sheets to protect tables or desks, or sponge/
        vacuum to clean

    Water in a pitcher or container(s) that can pour easily

    Optional: Soil enrichments: sand, peat moss, vermiculite
          Larger trays or flats, for cheerful beds of green

Suggestion: Choose seeds that are easy to grow (wheat, alfalfa, radish) so that children will see green soon. Try out more chancy herbs first. For a large group, have earth and seeds in plastic bags for each small group.

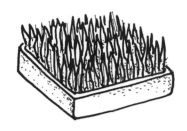

Preparation

As you initiate the project, talk about Lent as a time to prepare the earth to receive seeds of life. Farmers plow up the hard earth to receive seeds that will grow into the vegetables and other crops that will feed us and all the animals. Plowing up and preparing the soil is the first and most necessary step in a process that provides for most creatures on the planet. It is a life-giving process that reflects another that takes place in God's people during Lent.

Christian people prepare their minds and hearts to receive the seeds of God's life and love. They do this with prayer, fasting (eating less but healthier foods), and sharing more of what they have with others who are hungry or homeless.

Planting seeds helps you to see the life and happiness that come from an invisible process that takes place in your heart as you live a real Lent with Jesus and all God's people.

Doing the Craft

Place pebbles or gravel in the bottom of the container for drainage, then fill with potting soil, preferably mixed with small amounts of sand, peat moss, and/or vermiculite.

Plant the seeds at the proper depth. Wheat berries and alfalfa need only a light sprinkling of earth over them. Plant herb, flower, and vegetable seeds according to their directions.

Water the seeds so that the water penetrates to the bottom of the pot; keep it evenly moist without saturating the soil until the seeds begin to sprout.

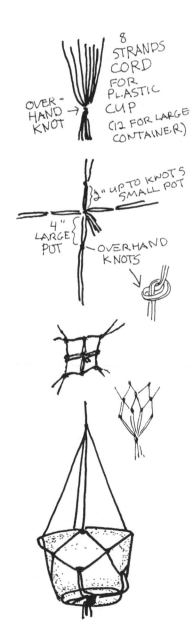

HANGING POT DIRECTIONS

Gather eight strands of cord or yarn and tie them all together in a loop knot one inch from one end. The extra inch will form a tassel. With the tassel at the center, spread out the rest of the string in twos, in north, south, east, and west directions. Tie each pair in a loop knot one to two inches away from the tassel, according to the size of your pot.

Separate each of your two strands in opposite directions, to meet its neighbor halfway between the last knot. Tie the two new partners in another loop knot one to two inches away from the last knot. Separate the new partners so that each strand will go back to its original partner; tie these together one to two inches away from the previous knot. Repeat separating and tying, then place the pot on the strings, centered on the tassel. Pull the strings together at the top and lift the cradle up to see if it safely holds your pot. If it doesn't, do more knotting; if it does, tie the ends together at the top and make a cord loop for hanging.

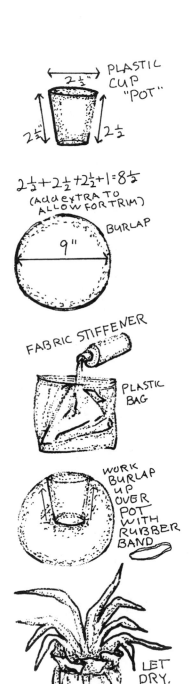

STATIONARY POTS

Decorate a pot to sit on a table or window with paper ribbon, burlap, or other fabric. Paper ribbon is simplest; choose a muted earthy color: brown, beige, or a muted blue. Cut a length long enough to wrap around your pot and leave decorative ends extending three to five inches. Paper ribbons are less shiny and festive than satin or grosgrain; save these for Easter.

BURLAP COVERS

A variation for any pot: wrap it all up in burlap—plain or treated with a fabric stiffener—then tie it with a cord or paper ribbon. Line it with plastic for pots that have drainage.

The burlap will give you an earthy feeling appropriate to Lenten work on the inner soil of the soul. Make it a reminder to live Lent fully and deeply, focused on the life, growth, and joy it will bring about.

Materials
Plastic cup or other pot
Burlap to cover
Cord or paper ribbon
Optional: Fabric stiffener, plastic bag, rubber band

Doing the Craft
Measure the sides and bottom of your pot to find how big the diameter of a burlap circle should be, then add two to three inches all around. Use a plate or pot lid that size to draw a big circle on the burlap, then cut it out. If you wish, put this in a plastic bag and pour on some fabric stiffener; work it through the burlap with your fingers.

Spread out the circle on newspaper or plastic, place the pot in the middle, and fold the circle up around the pot, gathering it toward the top. Work a rubber band up from the bottom toward the top, moving the burlap to get even gathers.

When the band gets close to the top, the edge of the burlap will be getting frayed and ragged; make it a little more so for an interesting border. Trim it evenly above the pot rim or make a neat fringe.

If you use a fabric stiffener, set the pot aside to dry overnight or speed up the process with a hair dryer. Later, remove the rubber band and replace it with a cord or paper ribbon.

SEWN POTS

Cut matching pieces of burlap and plastic large enough to wrap around your pot or plastic container, then add a half inch all around. Place them face to face, then sew them one-half inch in from the edges ALMOST all around. Leave four inches open so that you can turn it right side out, so that the seams face in.

Wrap around the pot and tie with paper ribbon, yarn, or cord, preferably in a natural, light beige color.

Variation

With careful sewing, the plastic-lined burlap becomes the pot itself. You need to make a paper pattern; use a box as a pattern or follow the diagrams in the margins. Form two identical pouches that you sew or glue together, one of burlap, seams inside, the other of plastic or oilcloth, seams outside. Place the liner inside the burlap. Cut the top of the liner so it is one-half to one inch shorter than the burlap; then fold the burlap top over it, and glue or sew down. Fabric stiffener will also hold everything in place.

Fill with soil, leaving at least an inch at the top. Plant your seeds or put in a plant cutting that has been rooted in water. Optional: Tie with cord or ribbon around the outside toward the top to draw the burlap in a little more to help keep the soil inside.

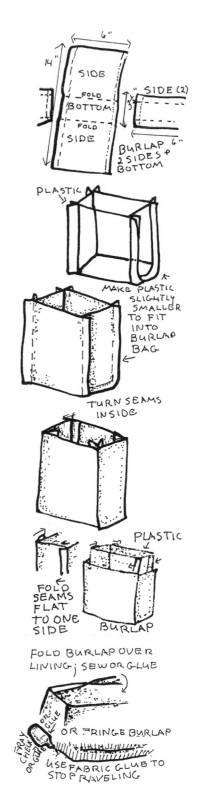

Wormhouses

Work on the soil of your inner garden is sometimes a little messy, but it is more than worth it. Often the more you are willing to get down to the nitty-gritty of what is going on inside you to see where you need to improve, the better the results.

Making wormhouses is a great project for people interested in the health of planet earth and the health of their own inner world. Wormhouses are safe, clean, and odorless if handled with a minimum of thought and care. They offer an opportunity for one person, family, or class to oversee—even in a small apartment or classroom—a complete recycling of something most people think of only as "smelly garbage." The bonus is an end product of great value: an excellent fertilizer.

For those adults who may shrink from touching worms, you can let the children do it. Schools all over the country are working with worm towns, using them to teach other subjects such as science and math. At New Jersey Earth Day exhibitions, worm towns drew excited groups of children and requests for return engagements.

WHEN IS A WORM BEAUTIFUL?

An art teacher once asked all his students to write a paragraph answering the question: When is a worm beautiful? His answer was, "To another worm." Those who create wormhouses, however, will have a different answer.

Worms create a compost that is extra nourishing to the growth of plants, flowers, vegetables, and crops—all the life that feeds and nourishes creatures of the planet. They do this by a natural process that provides many benefits and poses no dangers.

Worms eat garbage. They take the food parings, eggshells, coffee grinds, brown bananas, or outer lettuce leaves you used to throw away and work quietly, unobtrusively, to turn them into fertilizer for your houseplants, seed projects, gardens, and fields. Whatever you want to grow will do better with their help.

Cities and towns today don't know what to do with their garbage; a famous barge filled with it traveled at sea for months before it could dispose of its cargo. It is expensive to get rid of, even by burning, and burning causes pollution problems.

Worms, on the other hand, make something good of it. With the help of newspaper and a cup of plain garden soil, they create castings filled with tiny unseen forms of life, microbes and bacteria that make a richer, safer soil than chemicals can produce. Mass agribusiness raises pollution problems with runoff from chemical fertilizers and insect control. The fertilizer created by worm castings will never do that; it is safe, clean, and odorless if done properly.

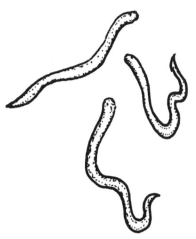

DEATH AND LIFE

While a wormhouse may not seem much compared to the huge landfills and gigantic agribusinesses, it is a little step, symbolic and practical, in the right direction. It is taking just a little time to "die to self," to help yourself and others—the kind of action asked for in Lent. It also is appropriate for the season in its preparation for and celebration of the return of life in nature from its apparent death.

In scripture and in popular thought, worms are associated with death and decay. But a wormhouse raises the question: When does death really occur? You can hardly tell; there is life going on during the whole process. The core of a once ripe red tomato, the parings of once living potatoes, the skins of once live apples growing on trees become food for worms and other organisms that turn them into a rich fertilizer. This fertilizer feeds seeds, plants, and trees that produce more tomatoes, potatoes, and apples. Even on the natural level, where all things seem to die, the cycle of life goes on.

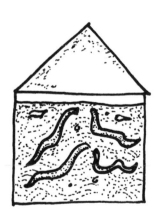

WORMHOUSE ART

A wormhouse can fit under your kitchen sink, in your hall closet, or in your basement; it may also be displayed as a work of art.

Challenge the imaginations of children to choose the kind of house it will be and its name: Worm Manor, Compost Condo, Annelid Apartments, etc. Newark children did a Worm Housing Development, a Worm Garbage Gourmet Shop, and a Wedding Chapel (from an old lamp shade and parts of soda bottles).

After children have a name, challenge them to make a house that will fit the name, interest and delight people from the outside, and keep the worms happy on the inside. The only design restrictions are the needs of the worms and where you want to display the house: the amount of space, the colors, etc.

Directions based on the needs of worms are given in the Introduction under "Earth Crafts," with more ideas to help you fire the imaginations of your young people.

Follow-Up Activities

Create a worm town as a Lenten or Whole Earth Day display. Show samples of the compost produced and healthy plants that are grateful for the work of the worms. Give prizes for the most imaginative, the most beautiful, the most inventive, the most scientific, and the funniest wormhouses.

Pray the "Blessing of a Wormhouse" that follows here. Combine with the growing prayers in Chapters 2 (on resolutions—tending to a wormhouse can be a resolution in itself) or 7.

Blessings of Wormhouses and Seeds

These prayers may also be adapted to bless seed pots and planters by using the proper names in the parentheses, wormhouses or seeds, and omitting what is not appropriate.

OPENING SONG: "All Things Bright and Beautiful," from *Rise Up and Sing,* Oregon Catholic Press, or "Let My Heart Be Good Seed," from *With One Voice*

OPENING COMMENTS: It's good to remember to thank God for all the wonderful things in creation that make up our lives. Sometimes even the tiniest, most overlooked things can remind us. Even (lowly worms, little seeds) have a place in praising God.

Today we will give thanks for the little (wiggly worms, or seeds) that live under the earth, working to keep our gardens growing. Worms make earth aerated and fertile so plants can produce their flowers and food.

(Worms, seeds) help us to remember that the littlest creatures are a gift of God. They remind us that the littlest, least appreciated jobs are important if they nurture life and love.

(Worms, seeds) tell us that no creature is too little or hidden to have a place in God's world. How much more important, then, is each precious human person, no matter how small, quiet, unnoticed, or overlooked.

No matter who we are, we all have a job to do to help both creation and other people. Each caring action, each smile, each kindness or good word helps God's life to grow in all of us. Little things matter.

The following, in parentheses, is for seeds only:

(Jesus insisted that the little children, the smallest of humans, be allowed to come close to him so that he could see their smiles, share their joy, hug them, and bless them.

Jesus knew they were very important in God's kingdom. He knew they were the seeds of the future. He knows that everyone here is also very important in God's kingdom and that each little thing they do to help people and life is precious. We can all be receptive to the love seeds God plants in us and help God to plant them in our world.)

READING: Psalm 104:24, 27-30

THE BLESSING OF WORMHOUSES: Lord God, loving creator of all life, we praise you and thank you for all your gifts of life.

You gave earth as a home to life and commanded it to bring forth its bounty to feed the hungry. You made sun and rain to call forth its growth, and little creatures to work in its soil for the good of all.

Bless this house (these houses) that we have made to aid and help the earth and its growing things. May it (they) help us grow in reverence and respect for all forms of life. May we use them gratefully for the good of all.

May our work to help life on earth be a reminder of our new life in Jesus, a life that will be ongoing forever. As we tend to the earth now, may we also tend to the gift of life you give us in Jesus, through whom we pray. Amen.

BLESSING OF SEEDS: Lord God, our loving creator, thank you for planting hidden seeds of your love in our hearts. Let the seeds we plant in earth help us to remember your hidden life in each of us and to nurture that life with prayer and kind actions.

Bless these seeds that they may grow well. May we understand their message and not forget your gifts to us. Bless all who are present that we may grow and flourish in your love, in Jesus, your son, in whom we pray. Amen.

SONG: "You Call Us to Live," or "Jesus You Love Us," or "Children of God," from *Calling the Children,* Oregon Catholic Press

CHAPTER 7

Growing Arts

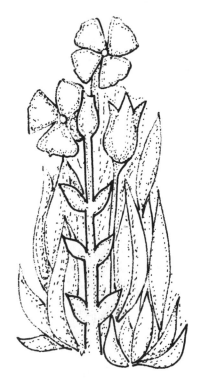

When I entertained the idea of including wormhouses in this book, parents of small boys assured me they would love it; others were not so sure. One friend who loved the *idea* said, "But do I have to really do the worms? Couldn't I just talk about them?"

Of course, there is nothing like an experience, and actually working directly with earth and worms gives new, fresh, and forceful insights into Lenten concepts of new life, plus direct help to plant life. However, if you don't want to work with worms directly and still want to grapple with the ideas in a craft, do it colorfully in drawing, painting, collage, or progressive banner making.

To inspire people, help them to recall their own growing experiences or tell them a story; one is included in this chapter, inspired by a gospel image. Practice telling this story, illustrating it as you go; a few lines will do it. Don't worry about the end product; remember, it's people and process that are important. You are communicating something of value, and that's what counts. Don't try to be Michelangelo. Unless you have a genius or two, your children can't draw as he did either. A simple effort on your part will leave them free to do their own interpretations.

Story: The Seeds That Grew

Once there were little seeds that had been buried in the earth all winter. There was a layer of snow to keep them warm, and most of the time they just slept, but now something was happening above their dark earth house to change things.

The sun in the sky was getting closer, and its warmth began to melt the snow, so that water trickled down into the earth. Soon, the little seeds were soaked. They didn't like this at all; their hard outer coats were getting softer and softer, until they began to split and fall away.

"My shell, my shell, it's almost gone. What will I do?" cried one of the little seeds.

"Mine is completely gone," cried another."

"This is awful," said a third.

One of the seeds, who had been hugging his hard shell, had rolled himself under a rock to stay dry. "I'm hanging on to mine," he said.

One of the very wet seeds noticed that the earth above was getting warmer. Something in him wanted to reach up to it. He stretched himself up, further and further, and some roots stretched down to support this push. Suddenly, a pale white sprout shot up from his top.

"Hey, look at that," said one of the other seeds. "How did he do it?"

"How does it feel?" asked another. "Does it hurt?"

"No, it feels wonderful," said the sprout. "Growing is great! I want to do it even more, it feels so good." With this, the sprout stretched again and got even bigger.

The other seeds, all except the dry one, joined him with enthusiasm, reaching and stretching with gusto, urging each other on. Soon they were all putting roots down, down, deeper into the earth, while pale white sprouts burst from their tops, reaching up, up, higher and higher.

But the one little seed that had stayed dry said, "I'm not going to let my hard shell go. You're all crazy."

After a while most of the sprouts rested after their hard work of growing, but not the first sprout. "I think there's something up there, more than what's here," he said. "That wonderful warmth, and there's a glimmer of something bright." He surged upward again.

The dry seed hugged his hard shell closer, worried that it was becoming a bit wrinkled now. He peered out from under his rock and cried, "You ninnies, this dark earth is all there is. Keep your shells on and make the most of it."

But the first sprout didn't even hear him; at that moment, he burst out of the dark earth into a wide open space with blue sky and sunshine. "Wow," he cried. "Color! Light! A whole different, wonderful world." He stretched out toward the sky and sprouted two large, beautiful, bright green leaves.

But now the other sprouts couldn't hear him, although some thought they heard a "Wow!"

The dry seed scoffed. "He's gone. I knew it. Gave up all this for some crazy idea about there being more!" He pulled back under the rock and bumped into another dry seed hiding under there, also holding onto its hard outer shell. "At least someone else has some sense besides me."

"Yeah," said his new friend. "They must be nuts to think there could be anything more when you can see the world is made up of dirt, nothing else."

Most of the young sprouts hesitated in their upward surge, afraid to go on and lose what they had. One, however, kept her head up and said, "I know that was a 'Wow!' I heard, and there was something about color and light. That warmth coming from up there is good. There is more; something inside me just knows it has to grow." She pushed up, and the moment her pale shoot went beyond the earth the others heard a joy-ful "OOOHhhhh!" and even caught a glimpse of brightness for just an instant.

Most of the sprouts rushed to join the first two in burst-ing out of the dark earth into the sunlight. Some came through with little leaves, some with green spears. They danced in the sunshine, and when a cloud came, they drank in the cooling rain it gave them. They grew and grew, until buds began to appear.

Down in the earth, underneath the stone, the dry seeds began to crumble away to dust, but above, in the sunlight, the seeds that grew waved their leaves happily in the fresh spring breeze. They grew and grew into strong green plants that budded and blossomed into flowers of many colors and shapes. Together they formed a beautiful garden. The sun seemed to shimmer around them in rainbow halos that radiated out from each toward all the others, until they met in the spaces between them and embraced in loving whispers: "Isn't it great? Aren't you glad? Praise God, who made us, whose warm love called us to grow. We gave up so little, those tiny hard shells, and look how we've grown! We've gained so much more."

Everyone who came to the garden was made happy by the fresh green, the flowers, and later by the fruits and vegetables that many of the little seeds now brought forth. People who took the time to look carefully could see those happy, loving rainbow halos radiating out from each plant toward all the others and toward the sun, and even toward themselves. It helped them to feel closer to everything and everyone and to want to grow and reach out themselves to discover all there is in God's wonderful creation.

ILLUSTRATING THE STORY

As you tell the story, illustrate with crayons to show the sun, the snow disappearing, the roots going down, the sprouts shooting up, the leaves spreading, and the plants going higher. Have fun with the bursting out of the flowers. When they reach the top of the paper, put down the crayons and pick up a brush.

Begin to outline each flower, to sort of halo it, with a brush stroke of paint, preferably a lighter color such as yellow, gold, pink, orange, or red. Give all the crayon strokes an outline on either side. Wash the brush and lay another "halo" of color next to the first one all around, then repeat with another color. Continue until the outlines meet in the middle of the spaces between the flowers; this will give the picture richness and excitement, and you don't have to be an artist to do it!

CRAYONS, MARKERS, AND WATERCOLORS

These simple techniques can help your children firm up Lenten concepts of new life. The techniques will also give them better eye-hand coordination skills, necessary for reading and learning skills, as they grow in faith.

Materials

Construction, drawing, or watercolor paper
Crayons
Watercolor or tempera paints, with brush, water, and paper towels
OR magic markers/watercolor markers.

Preparation

For watercolors or tempera, see "Painting" in the techniques section of the Introduction to this book.

Doing the Craft

Have children draw their own versions of seeds growing into flowers and fruit, beginning with crayon. Ask them to show the glory of the life that God gives to all creatures, plants as well as animals, by adding halos, outlining them with a brush and paint or with markers.

When their drawings have been completed, plan to give them a compliment that gently, unobtrusively furthers the meaning of the story. Hang up the works of art or give them a prominent place for a time of prayer and say: "Look at what wonderful pictures we've done to show how giving up a little bit during Lent can help us grow and experience good things." Jesus said, "Unless the grain of wheat falling into the ground dies, it remains alone, but if it dies, it brings forth much fruit."

Further Activities

Draw heavy lines on paper or tagboard with crayons, then cover the whole drawing with glowing gold and yellow, or orange and pink, coats of watercolor, for a crayon resist.

Ask children to act out or dance the seed story by scrunching down like seeds under the earth, sending up little sprouts with their hands, then growing up to a standing position and spreading out arm

"Saints, legendary artists, poets, composers, inventors and spiritual leaders illustrate the gains that society accrues when people develop their spiritual life— their inmost animating energies, drives and awarenesses. . . . Whether we believe in destiny, God, or our inner, higher power, as we nurture and productively express our talents, fascinations and inner realities, we bring fresh ideas and our own enhanced presence into being . . . we serve progress . . . no matter how seemingly insignificant our abilities."
— Marsha Sinetar
A Way without Words

branches that sway in the fresh spring breezes. Make flower hats for them to put on when they are "fully grown."

Pray the seed and growing prayers at the end of this chapter, or in Chapter 2 or 6.

MAGAZINE COLLAGE

Have children go through magazines and tear out swatches of color to create a design that shows plant life springing out of dark earth up to greet a blue sky, sun, and rain, and bursting into bloom. Do this in one project, or progressively, according to the sequence described for "Seed Growing Banner" that follows. See the "Paper Crafts" section in the Introduction for instructions.

Saying "Yes!"
Flowers and/or Leaves

Materials
>   Construction paper
>   Scissors, glue sticks, staplers, hole punch
>   Yarn/string
>   Crayons and markers
>   A beautiful branch standing upright in a container weighed down
>   with sand or rice
>   Optional: The flower patterns in this chapter

Preparation
Say, in your own words: "All year long, but especially during Lent, we are given many invitations and opportunities to grow in God's life and love. What God needs is our wholehearted, cheerful 'YES!' Because we grow through difficult as well as happy times, we sometimes need to ask God's help to have a positive attitude and to trust that things will be better."

To help everyone remember this, ask them to make one or more flowers (and/or leaves) with a hanging loop. You may also ask them to write on the back ways that they have been asked by God to grow in the past and whether or not they said "YES!" If they didn't seize the opportunity, the flower will help them to do so next time; if they did,

Saying "Yes!" Flowers

Use as patterns to cut from construction paper, or make your own designs. You can also color and cut these!

Reminders to say "Yes!" to God's invitations to grow

If you wish, write on the flowers ways God calls you to grow, and write your "Yes!" too.

©Jeanne Heiberg 1996

it will be a celebration. Use the flowers or leaves in a ritual action during the "Litany of Growing Prayer" that follows or with the growing prayer in Chapter 5.

Doing the Craft

Form the flower or leaf by a construction paper collage or by drawing with crayon or marker. Cut out each flower and attach a string/yarn loop through a punched hole or by stapling.

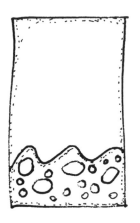

PROGRESSIVE BANNERS

Nature itself helps you to celebrate Lent and Easter, but you can bring its message into higher focus with a progressive banner. Patterns are provided for you to enlarge to suit your needs, to build on, or to encourage you to do your own designs. And after telling the seed story, who knows what inspirations and art your children may provide!

You may want to do the finished banner background and pieces yourself and let everyone see the work grow. Add a bit more every week, with a Lenten reflection.

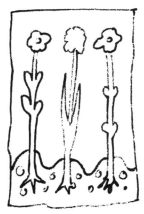

You may want to make it a family, friends, or class project to involve everyone as much as possible. The added time that cutting, gluing, or sewing takes, plus adding to the banner throughout a season, is all to the good in the faith-building aims of this book. The activity itself is saying, "Prepare the soil of your heart and mind. Receive the seeds of God's word and see the growth of a garden, representing God's new life."

Your people will become more involved with the idea, so they can live it more fully and be reminded of it during the rest of the year as they admire what they have made together. You can bet that the faith idea the work expresses will remain with them; not only the banner will grow, but the people as well. More ideas to motivate and teach your group can be found in the preceding chapter and in the section on Lent in the Introduction. See the "Cloth Arts" section in the Introduction for the practical choices to be made in materials and methods.

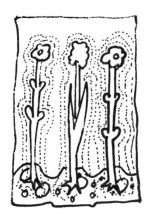

Materials

A length of blue cloth a little larger than you want the finished banner to be (or felt in the exact size)

A backing piece

The following cloth swatches: dark brown for earth; gray for pebbles, stones, possibly rain; ochre or gold for bulbs/seeds and

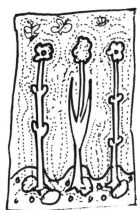

Growing Banner

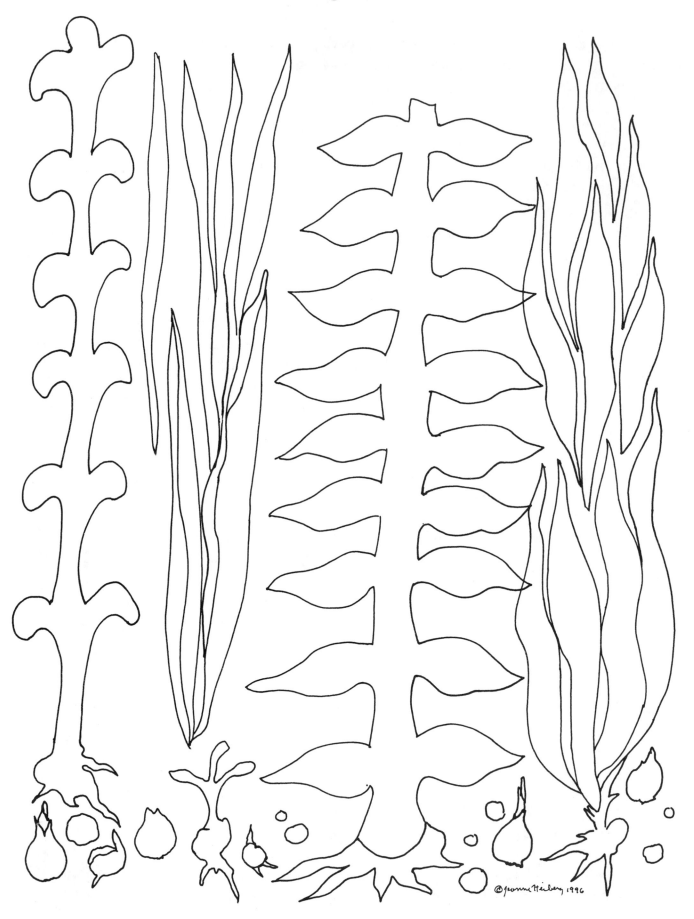

roots; white for snow and clouds; yellow and orange for sun, butterflies, flowers; yellow and bright green for sprouts turning into stems and leaves (try mixing many shades of green—yellowish, silvery, turquoise greens ranging from light to dark); many more bright colors for flowers: red, pink, magenta, orange, lavender, and purple; and white, yellow, and orange butterflies

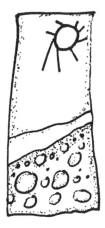

See "Cloth Arts" in the Introduction for other supplies, choices, and methods. Have all the pieces ready to add by the time you plan to introduce them.

Building the Banner

Start with just the brown earth, several inches deep, possibly under a smaller layer of snow that you can remove later. Slant the earth or give it some ups and downs to make it interesting. Add some rocks or pebbles if you wish. Then place seeds or bulbs in this section.

In the second week of Lent add a warm sun, and later, a cloud and possibly a few gray slanting lines to indicate rain. Take away the layer of snow. Next, add roots growing down from the seeds/bulbs and a few shoots going up. Add a longer green stem and two leaves above the ground.

As Lent progresses, the banner does also. Add longer stems and more leaves, with variety: tulip and daffodil spears, almond or heart-shaped leaves for other flowers.

Toward Easter, add buds, birds, and ladybugs. At the very end, add big, bold, beautiful flowers, butterflies, and any other spring things you and your young people want.

As people cut and paste/sew this banner, as they add roots and sprouts to seeds, then stems, leaves, and flowers over a period of several weeks, they will become increasingly involved with faith concepts of dying and rising and of growing in God, in Jesus, and in his new life. They will not forget concepts connected with such colorful, absorbing, fun things to do.

BANNER BLESSING

After all your work on the banner, it will deserve a blessing so that the spiritual reality it expresses will remain in the consciousness of those who took part in its creation.

Growing Banner

OPENING SONG: "How Great Thou Art"

LEADER: The Lord has called us together for a good work that will remind all who see it of God's gifts. It is fitting to praise and thank God for sharing his creative power with us and speaking through us in a visual work.

LEADER: The response to our prayers will be: YOUR WORKS, O LORD, ARE GREAT AND GLORIOUS.

 Rejoice in God and all his works: RESPONSE.
 Praise God for colors and textures: RESPONSE.
 Praise God for lines and shapes: RESPONSE.
 Praise God for symbols and signs: RESPONSE.
 Praise God for fabrics and threads: RESPONSE.
 Praise God for music and dance: RESPONSE.
 Praise God for arts and crafts: RESPONSE.
 Praise God for works that express his truth: RESPONSE.
 Praise God for endowing us with creativity: RESPONSE.
 Praise God for all the gifts Christ won: RESPONSE.

PRAYER: Lord, God, our creator, we give you thanks and praise for creating us in your own image, as children are made in the image of their parents. As your children, you call us to be partners with you in loving and in creating.

We have built this work of fabric art in memory of Jesus and his teaching. We ask you now to bless this banner, that it may be for us a sign of your love and a reminder of who we really are: your children, members of your family, one with you and one another in him. May all who see this work be lifted up to you in mind and heart as it speaks your word to them. May it be a constant joy and blessing to all.

We ask your blessing also on the people who worked to bring this banner into being. Give them joy and enthusiasm to go on growing in you. Help them to share your message in word and image, and in actions of kindness and love. Whatever they do, may it be for your honor and glory and their peace and happiness. We ask this in Jesus, who won for us all good things. Amen.

Litany of Growing Prayer

Make a template or form (such as the one described below) so that people can write their own litany words in the blank spaces. The form will give the prayers unity and help everyone to know when to give their response.

To motivate, ask people what has helped them to grow, love, learn, and be happy. The beautiful things they love in nature are reminders of how wonderful it is to grow. Remind them that food helps them to grow, but so do smiles; kind, caring actions; and learning, especially about God's love.

Kind, helpful things people do bring growth, along with good, brave actions. Forgiving, making up after a fight or hurt, learning from mistakes, sticking to a difficult task or Lenten resolutions, working through a disappointment: these are some of the best growing times, as long as you remember God's love and ask God's help.

Ask people to decorate their template after they write the words so that the person who reads it will be doubly inspired. You can have people read their own prayer, exchange them so that everyone reads someone else's, or give them all to one reader.

SAMPLE LITANY TEMPLATE

Write in your own words ways you grow in God's love.
FOR _____ (leave two to three lines) _____ THANK YOU LORD.
RESPONSE: LORD, HELP US TO GROW IN YOUR LIFE.

Other choices for a litany template:
"Loving God, you help us to grow by _____. Thank you, Lord."
RESPONSE: HELP US TO GROW IN YOUR LOVE.

OR

"Loving God, you invite us to grow by_____. Thank you for chances to love and learn."
RESPONSE: MAY WE SAY "YES!" TO YOUR CALLS TO GROW.

Materials and Preparations

Use the litany templates to gather prayers from all participants, then consolidate them into five to eight petition prayers, avoiding repetition and considering age and attention span. Use them during the "Litany Prayer."

Have people make flowers/leaves in advance with a loop for hanging. Prepare a beautiful bare branch large enough to hold everyone's flowers. Prepare a prayer table with something alive and growing on it (or photos), plus a bible, candles, and a cross.

OPENING SONG: "As the Sun with Longer Journey" or "The Word of God Is Source and Seed," from *With One Voice*, Augsburg Fortress

OPENING PRAYER: Loving God, you give us many ways to grow in your life. We want to learn to see them and seize each opportunity. Help us to find joy in your calls to grow. Guide each one present to be the beautiful person, created in your image, that you intended. Our response to these litany prayers will be: _____
(the response on the template you gave to your people).
(Read the litanies and ask everyone to join in the response.)

PRAYER: Creator God who gives life and growth to all, receive our spoken and unspoken prayers. Bring these prayers and those who pray them into a fulfillment even more wonderful than anyone can imagine as we grow in your life. We ask this in him who came to teach us how to grow, Jesus, your son. Amen.

RITUAL ACTION: It is exciting to discover the many ways God gives people to grow. You can even learn from mistakes and difficult things, as well as from joys and happy times.

As a sign of readiness to say yes to God's invitations, you are invited to bring your flower/leaf and place it on this bare branch. As the branch fills with flowers, you will see how much more alive it becomes, as we do, when we say "YES!" to God's invitations to grow.

CLOSING PRAYER: Creator God, who gives life and growth to all on earth, may your presence in our hearts and minds become like a garden or a flourishing field. As this bare branch has been transformed, so also may we, and far more, with the joy and glory of your abundant life. Amen.

SONG: "Inch by Inch, Row by Row," by Pete Seeger, or "Now the Green Blade Rises," *Lutheran Book of Worship*, Augsburg Fortress. See the music section at the end of the book.

Baptism into New Life

The life-giving water of baptism is a major theme of Lent that dovetails with others already outlined. Water turns the desert into a garden, so it connects with the desert retreat, readying the soil, growing, and from death to life. Related signs of light, oil, the white garment, the victorious cross, and, most of all, belonging to God's people have echoes in the ending of separation, healing, unity, sacrifice, renewal in God's life and presence, and other themes.

Baptismal themes are so strong because Lent grew backward from the Easter vigil to prepare catechumens for the initiation that took place on that most holy of nights. It is still the ideal time for the final preparation of adults for baptism, and a time for all to renew in themselves what it means to be baptized. To utilize a craft in this preparation or renewal will give color and body to the ideas.

An outline of baptismal symbols and patterns, with a brief overview of their meaning, follows. This can be drawn on for Lenten collages, banners, and quilts. You may want people to interpret symbols in their own way or use the designs for quilts, banners, and paper collages. Themes may be expressed quickly in a drawing/painting or worked in felt or woven fabrics, as described in "Cloth Arts" in the Introduction.

Symbols of Baptism

WATER: The key sign for baptism and a major theme for Lent. Everything needs water to live. The desert is barren, void of life, because water is lacking; rain brings immediate growth and blossoming. Gardens are lush and beautiful when there is an abundance of water. Water refreshes, cleans, renews, and gives life to people and their planet, Earth.

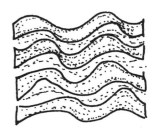

Humans need water to live. Food can be eliminated for a long time and people survive, but they can live only a short period without water. Human bodies are 85 to 90 percent water. Pure fresh water and vegetables that thrive on water are essential to good health.

There is a death element in water; large amounts of it can drown you. The water of baptism, however, says that you die to sin, self-centeredness, and separation from God. You are then free to begin a new God-centered life in Christ.

FISH AND SHELL: Baptismal symbols that go with water. John the Baptist is often pictured baptizing Jesus with a shell. In the Middle Ages, a hat with a shell was the sign of a pilgrim, someone on a journey to better live his or her baptismal faith.

Fish exist in water, just as Christians exist in a sea of God's love. You experience more and more of this love as you overcome your separation from God and others. Jesus overcame this separation in his victory of the cross, and that victory is extended to you by baptism.

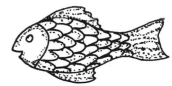

PLANTS, FLOWERS, AND TREES: Signs of the new, abundant life that Jesus won and that Christians enter into through baptism. The theme of spring growth relates to the sacrament as well as to resurrection. Plant life cannot germinate, put down roots, and send up sprouts, leaves, flowers, and fruit without water. The water of baptism that initiates people into the continuous flow of life from God to human beings is necessary to growth in the Spirit.

THE CHRISTIAN ASSEMBLY—OTHER CHRISTIANS: With water, a key sign of baptism. As individuals are baptized into Christ, they are also baptized into the body of Christ, the church, the people of God. Each time Christians come together, they are a sign of baptism, the end of separation and the belonging in family unity with God and others. A more recent addition to baptismal symbolism, the Christian assembly has been elevated to a primary sign, equal to water in importance.

LIGHTED CANDLE: Like the sun or fire, a sign of God's presence. A lighted candle is given to all baptized persons as a sign of God's presence in their lives. Now they belong to the light; God wants to shine in their consciousness with wisdom, knowledge, and understanding.

Signs of Baptism

Use copier to enlarge each symbol to fit a five-inch square or to a size of your choice.

Shell
and
Water

Oil

Living Waters

White Robe

©Jeanne Heiberg 1996

Candle

New Life

Oil

Fish

Bible

Assembly

©Jeanne Heiberg 1996

Cross

Bible

Shell

Love

New Life

Light

© Jeanne Heiberg 1996

No longer stumbling blindly in darkness and fear, Christians are welcomed into God's light and love. Along with water, all things need light to grow. Human beings need the light of God's presence to grow, a vision of God's love to live by.

Jesus said, "I am the light of the world." He also said to his apostles, "You are the light of the world," extending this function to all who truly live their baptism.

OIL: A human necessity for physical nutrition and healing, and a sign of the Holy Spirit, source of spiritual nourishment and healing. Machinery needs oil to overcome friction and run smoothly. The human body needs some healthy fats also to smooth along its functions. The human community as a whole needs the oil of the Holy Spirit to overcome emotional friction and function smoothly and harmoniously in a unified way.

In spite of cholesterol scares and exhortations to eat less fat, small amounts are necessary in the diet. Cold pressed olive oils are especially healthy. Biblical foods and healing ointments were largely made from them. In the hot, dry climate of Palestine, ointments made from such oils also gave protection to the exposed skin of face, hands, and feet, just as God's love nourishes and protects when people are exposed to the vicissitudes of life.

Kings, prophets, and special messengers were anointed with perfumed oils for their mission. *The Christ* means "the anointed one." Jesus has a key mission to all human beings, but each Christian shares in that mission.

During the ritual, the celebrant anoints the baptized person with oil to show that they belong to Christ and share in his kingship and prophetic mission. They are called to discover their inner Christ life and become a sign of God's presence on earth.

WHITE ROBE: A sign of the new life—the pure, sinless, fresh start in life—for the person baptized into Christ. It is a longstanding tradition to wrap the newly baptized person in a brand new white garment.

Now a baby is brought to church in a christening dress or presented with a white bib, symbolic of the robe. Early Christian adults, however, were re-dressed, after baptism by immersion, in a white garment lovingly sewn by established members of the community. So dressed, the newest members were confirmed, received their first eucharist, and took their place in the community.

A garment is an external expression of who we are. In the last book of the New Testament, both angels and the saints in heaven are described as wearing white robes. A white baptismal robe establishes a Christian as a citizen of heaven, forgiven, renewed, loved by God, and privileged to live in a loving community of God's people.

CROSS: The standard of Christianity, given as a sign to a person during the rite of baptism. In the early Christian church, a cross was presented to each candidate during the process of initiation and preparation for the ritual. See Chapter 4, "The Victorious Cross," for more on this important sign.

BIBLE: The word of God plays an important part in preparing adults for baptism, in the rite itself, and in continued faith education over a lifetime.

In many churches, candidates for baptism are formally presented with a bible to impress on them the importance this book will play in their lives. This practice is often extended to children when they are old enough to study and begin to understand its contents.

Lent is a time to become more familiar with this basic book of faith and to help children listen to, act out, draw, and love the wonderful stories and values that the bible offers people of all ages.

Quilts/Banners

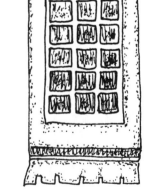

Quilting is a great art about which whole books of instructions have been written. For more traditional methods, please go to these; your library or bookstore is likely to have some or be able to obtain them for you.

The baptismal quilt described here requires only the materials and methods described in "Paper Crafts" and "Cloth Arts." However, some planning will help this project run smoothly.

Preparation

Make a rough estimate of how many people will contribute to the quilt and how large each individual square to be worked on will be. For nine people, you may want to plan for three squares across and three down; for twelve people, go to four down.

If the squares are to be five inches, plus an inch of space between each, your background must be at least twenty inches wide; add on the width of any borders for both sides. You can frame your quilt with strips of varying widths in solid colors or with prints, stripes, dots, zig-zags, etc.

For nine people the quilt will be the same length, unless you want wider borders or framing/hanging tabs at the top and bottom. A little more border at the bottom sometimes balances things out better. For twelve people doing five-inch squares, three across and four down, you will need a background at least twenty-five inches long, plus borders. With more people, plan on a bigger background.

Vary this planning to allow for: people making more than one square; more or fewer people; or bigger squares. You may want to form a large banner out of the nine by twelve inch squares sold precut in craft and fabric stores. This is no problem; figure it into your plan.

For Lent, you may want to plan a quilt using the designed squares in the four corners to form a cross made by empty space running through the middle. Figure out how much space you will need in each corner and how wide the cross will be, then add it all up with the borders.

Calico and other prints are often juxtaposed with solids for quilts; try this for yours, if you work in woven fabrics. Or combine fabric and felt. Have a group make squares or rectangles in solid-color felts with purple and turquoise backgrounds. Place these on a calico background of purple, with a contrasting calico in turquoise for the border. Add more border with ribbon in a different width, possibly a red, green, or deep blue grosgrain; or cut borders of cloth or felt.

Blues and greens with touches of yellow and spring colors are appropriate for baptism. Experiment with small pieces for your color scheme before undertaking a large one. Work out the size of squares, borders, etc., on a smaller scale. Use one inch on paper to every foot of the final quilt or get an architectural ruler for a wide choice of scales to work with.

Developing the Craft

Distribute squares of paper, felt, or cloth to people for backgrounds and more in different colors, even scraps, for designs. Provide patterns and/or ideas. Have people form one or more squares by cutting out the design and playing with it until they like it, then gluing or stitching the design to their square.

Have people place their finished squares on the background if it is ready, or on the cloth that will become the background later, so that they can see the unity that results. Point out the wonderful things that

can be accomplished when people work creatively together in peace and harmony.

The background piece may be finished, ready, and waiting or made up later, according to the directions in "Cloth Arts" in the Introduction to this book.

FOR A CLASS, CHURCH, OR BAPTISMAL PARTY

Though this banner can be made by one person, it is an ideal group project for a family, class, or group of friends.

With a group, ask all people taking part to choose one of the baptismal symbols pictured here to use as a pattern or as an inspiration for their own design. They are to cut out the pieces in cloth or felt (or paper for a collage), then glue (felt and paper) or sew it onto a five by five inch square. You can enlarge the patterns with a copier as long as you enlarge the background squares in the same ratio.

You may also have people only pin their work and baste it (sew with big quick stitches) or use a glue stick or light dabs of glue to tack their design onto a small background square. Have ready a volunteer (or a few) with a love for sewing to machine stitch the pieces on all the squares and sew the squares to the background that he or she, or another dedicated person, makes. Adults and students together will take pride in what results.

A teacher or parent may also prepare a permanent background that will hold squares that correspond to the usual number of children in a class. When baptism is studied, ask children to choose a symbol, cut out the pieces, and paste them on a small square of construction paper or felt. Finish them in one of the ways described in "Cloth Arts" in the Introduction.

Pin the finished pieces to the background for a few weeks or till the end of the year, then return them to the people who made them. You will be able to use the background next year, and your children will have a beautiful reminder of what they learned.

There are many approaches to group work. A family or class can work on the quilt when they get together and have it ready for Easter or for baptisms that will take place at or after Easter.

If you know someone with a baby to be baptized, or have one yourself, make it memorable for all, including the baby, with a quilt the child can carry into adulthood. Send friends/family members a quilt kit with what is needed for one square; it all fits easily into an envelope.

Assemble a set of one each: a paper pattern (made on a copier, let them cut it out), a square of material for the background, another smaller piece (or two) of material for the designs, and instructions. As an extra bonus, you may even want to include a needle (which you can use to pin the fabric together) and thread.

Also specify how and when you want the square to be returned: in a return envelope, brought to the baptism to be assembled at the party afterwards, or by a certain date.

At a party after the baptism, place the squares on a piece of background cloth so that everyone can see how their contribution fits into a whole quilt. Finish it later and present it as a beautiful gift to the infant or adult baptized. See directions under "Cloth Arts" in the Introduction.

The patterns you send may vary. You may include those in this book, or you may have everyone do just one pattern, such as a heart. Something easy like this may even be precut in cloth, a bunch at a time, several thicknesses deep; do the same with the background squares. Choose several heart colors that will be repeated throughout the quilt for a nice rhythmic unity.

Put one heart, background square, needle, thread, and note in each envelope. Putting the kit together is such a small thing to do; it won't take up much time, and each person will contribute to something beautiful and meaningful for the baptized person and his or her family.

BAPTISMAL QUILT POEM AND PRAYER

Dear friend (Aunt Mary, Cousin George, etc.),
What looks like only simple fabric (or paper) here,
Is something you can make to bring us cheer;
A pattern you can sew onto a square, to be
A gift of hope, a handmade prayer.
It will become, when fashioned from the heart,
Sewn with your love, a most important part
Of something bigger, that says, tangibly,
To our newborn, "You're family,
Part of God's people, and ours too.
Dear child, we warmly, warmly welcome you."

ASSEMBLING PRAYER FOR
CLASS OR BAPTISMAL PARTY

To adapt the following prayer to a classroom session on baptism, change the baby references.

For a baptism party, keep a prayer ritual short and simple; pick out the parts you like best from the following or compose your own. Add peaceful taped music if you wish.

PRAYER: Loving God, you bring us into the life of your son, Jesus, in baptism, and in him promise a life that will never end. You bring us into one family, one in which we all play an important part. As we assemble each piece of a quilt to form a whole work of art, help us to remember that you need each of us to receive and share your love. Give each of us joy in forming this quilt and in helping to build up your kingdom of love, in companionship with Jesus and with one another. Amen.

COMMENTARY: We have come together to celebrate a new member in our family and a new member of God's kingdom. Many of you have added to our happiness this day by completing a small square that is to become part of a larger baptismal quilt, or banner, to fix this day in memory, and teach our child in future years.

Through this quilt, ___(baby or person's name, or you)___ will know that he/she is part of something wonderful; that together, in love and sharing, we all help to build up God's kingdom; and that baptism gives us a blanket of love to protect us on our earthly journey through the care of family, friends, church community, and good people everywhere.

As we each work on the little square of life that God gives us, as we did on the squares of the quilt, we help the blanket of protection and love to grow. Our squares of life are different, according to our families and friends, resources, responsibilities, talents and dreams; yet when we put them together with others, in peace and unity, something wonderful is created. The quilt will help us to remember this.

We want the putting together of the quilt to be a prayer, for the baby and for all of us, that we may all live out our baptism well and live as God meant us to, as people of light, peace, love, hope, promise, and joy.

Pray quietly on your own for a while, and when you feel ready, quietly place your square on the quilt wherever you wish. The aesthetics can be reworked later, but your loving prayer, in this symbolic action, is what is needed now.

(Play meditative music. When the banner is assembled:)

BLESSING OF THE QUILT, THE BABY, AND ALL ASSEMBLED:
Lord, you call us into your kingdom of love, a kingdom represented by this symbolic quilt, on which many of us worked with love. Bless this work of our hands; through it may we recall your gifts and joyfully pass the knowledge of them on to ___(baby's name)___ . May we remember that each one of us is important in your kingdom, a precious member of your family. May it remind us to be open to your gifts and generous in sharing your love with one another so that your kingdom will flourish and many more may come into its protection and comfort, its creativity and joy.

Bless ___(child's name)___ with the knowledge that he/she is loved always, by you and us. Keep him/her always under your loving protection, and ours, so that he/she may grow and flourish as a member of our family, and yours.

Bless all who are gathered here. The quilt shows many separate parts becoming one. May it symbolize a oneness that is among us so that _____ may be welcomed into a loving community, and learn that you are a gentle, caring God by the peace and joy he/she sees in all of us.

We ask this through him in whom we are baptized into your life, Jesus, your son. Amen.

Music

Although this book emphasizes visual arts and crafts, areas sometimes neglected in education and liturgy, music is still an important part of both; it works hand in glove with other arts to bring learning to life.

Included here are songs composed by Nelly Brown Bunk. One, "Good-bye Alleluia," was done in cooperation with the author and especially for this book. Others have been used in her parish of St. Thomas, Delmar, New York, with children's liturgies and prayers.

Paulist Press publishes *Songs for Young Children,* by Mary Lu Walker, with "The Flower Song," "Seeds of Hope," "Forest Trees," and "The Butterfly Song" for Growth, and for Resolutions and Social Justice, "Things That Money Can't Buy," "I Am Sorry," "Gathered Together in Love," and "Put On Love."

Other songs may be found in the spring/Lent edition or the music edition of *Today's Missal,* issued by the Oregon Catholic Press, Portland, Oregon. The *Lutheran Book of Worship* and a newer supplement, *With One Voice,* treasuries of Protestant songs, are available from Augsburg Fortress, 426 South Fifth Street, Minneapolis, Minnesota 55440. Your church or religious affiliation is sure to have favorite hymnbooks and sources you will also want to draw on.

Hi God 1, 2 and *3* have been popular for children, and *4* will be available when this book of crafts appears. There are other songbooks for children from Oregon Catholic Press, and the publisher was kind enough to provide me with the following list of songs appropriate to the themes in this book.

Growing

"You Call Us to Live," "Jesus You Love Us," "Children of God," by Christopher Walker, from *Calling the Children* and *Rise Up and Sing;* "All Things Bright and Beautiful," by Laura Wasson, from *Rise*

Up and Sing; "Friends Are Like Flowers" and "God Has Made Us a Family" from *Hi God 3,* by Carey Landry; and from *Hi God 4,* "Building the Kingdom."

Making Resolutions

"The Lord Is with You," by Anne Quigley, and "Forgiveness Prayer," by Regina Pirruccello, from *Rise Up and Sing;* "Take the Word of God with You," from *Calling the Children,* by Christopher Walker; "If Today You Hear God's Voice" and "Venimos (We Come)," by Mark Friedman, from *God Shines On You;* "Children of Tomorrow, Children of Today" and "Building the Kingdom," by Carey Landrey, from *Hi God 4;* and "Yes, Lord, Yes," from *Hi God 2.*

Social Justice

"Walk On," by Regina Pirruccello, "Welcome to the Kingdom," by Barbara Bridge, and "A Circle of Love," by Felicia Sandler, from *Rise Up And Sing;* "These Are Our Gifts," by Janct Vogt, "Venimos (We Come)," by Mark Friedman, from *God Shines on You;* "The Good News of Salvation," by Christopher Walker, from *Calling the Children;* "Children of Tomorrow, Children of Today" and "Building the Kingdom," from *Hi God 4,* and "We Are the Body of Christ," from *Hi God 2,* by Carey Landry.

Good-bye Alleluia   Nelly Brown Bunk

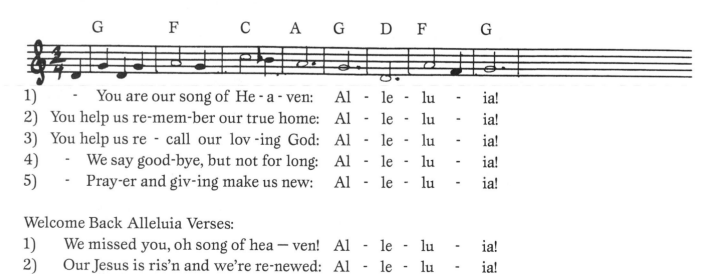

| G | F | C | A | G | D | F | G |

1)   -   You are our song of He‑a‑ven: Al ‑ le ‑ lu ‑ ia!
2)   You help us re‑mem‑ber our true home: Al ‑ le ‑ lu ‑ ia!
3)   You help us re ‑ call our lov‑ing God: Al ‑ le ‑ lu ‑ ia!
4)   -   We say good‑bye, but not for long: Al ‑ le ‑ lu ‑ ia!
5)   -   Pray‑er and giv‑ing make us new: Al ‑ le ‑ lu ‑ ia!

Welcome Back Alleluia Verses:
1)   We missed you, oh song of hea — ven!   Al ‑ le ‑ lu ‑ ia!
2)   Our Jesus is ris'n and we're re‑newed: Al ‑ le ‑ lu ‑ ia!
3)   We're children of heaven in Jesus' life: Al ‑ le ‑ lu ‑ ia!

Lord, Help Us to Grow
Nelly Brown Bunk

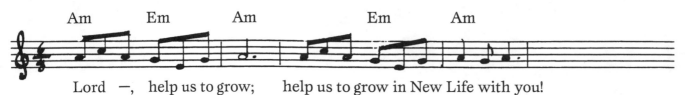

Lord —, help us to grow; help us to grow in New Life with you!

Quiet Song
Nelly Brown Bunk

Group 1 Shh! Shh! Op-en your heart. Shh! Shh! Let Je-sus in.

Group 2 Qui-et! Qui-et! heart. Qui-et! Qui-et! Let Je-sus in.

Lenten Song (from Psalm 50) # Psalm 50, alt.
Nelly Brown Bunk

Refrain: Have mercy on me, O Lord, my God, have mercy on me, O God.

Verse 1: Have mer-cy on me in your good — ness; in your tenderness, free me from sin.

I know that I sadden you when I do wrong, and I want to change my ways.

(to refrain)

Verse 1:
Have mercy on me in your goodness,
In your tenderness, free me from sin.
I know that I sadden you when I do wrong,
And I want to change my ways.

Verse 2:
A pure heart create in me, O God,
And make my spirit strong.
Give me again the joy of your help,
And I will sing your praise.